PE
PERFORMANCE

ZEN AND THE SPORTING ZONE

Felicity Heathcote was the official psychologist to the
Olympic Council of Ireland. She has worked with
many of Ireland's top sports personalities and her
contribution to the Irish Olympic team at Barcelona
in 1992 (particularly the boxers) has been highly
regarded. Her intention is to incorporate Zen thought
into western psychotherapeutic methods, especially in
the field of competitive sports at the highest level.

To my teachers, William Johnston SJ, Iwasa Sensei and Ustad Abdolrasouli who guided me, each in their own Way, along the neverending path to Perfection of Action

PEAK PERFORMANCE

ZEN AND THE SPORTING ZONE

Felicity Heathcote

WOLFHOUND PRESS

First published 1996 by
WOLFHOUND PRESS Ltd
68 Mountjoy Square
Dublin 1

and Wolfhound Press (UK)
18 Coleswood Rd
Harpenden
Herts AL5 1EQ

British Library Cataloguing in Publication Data
A catalogue record for this book is available from the British Library.

ISBN 0 86327 526 5

Typesetting: Wolfhound Press
Cover design: Slick Fish Design, Dublin
Printed in the Republic of Ireland by Colour Books Ltd., Dublin.

CONTENTS

Foreword   7

ZEN IN THE WAYS

1. The beginning of the journey   11
2. The martial arts   26
3. The artistic expression of Zen   41
4. The art of perfection in daily life   53

THE ZONE IN SPORT

5. Zen in water sports   67
6. Zen in general sports   82
7. Zen in team sports   98

THE TECHNIQUES

8. Mental training programmes   113
9. Application of the programme and results   137

10. Conclusion   170
11. Barcelona Olympics 1992   176

Notes   184
Glossary   189

Acknowledgements

My thanks first of all to my husband, Dr Niall Holohan, without whose support and unending patience this project could not have been completed.

Also to my two children, Clare and Andrew, who made sure I stayed grounded at all times.

To the members of the Olympic Council of Ireland – expecially President Pat Hickey, Vice-President Dermot Sherlock and Barry Houlihan – for their constant support of my ideas.

To Carole Walsh, whose integrity and outstanding dedication to Irish swimming are well known and whose help and advice were invaluable for the completion of this book.

To Yoshiko Ushioda, Curator of Japanese Art at the Chester Beatty Library in Dublin, and Dr Hiro Ueki of the United Nations for their expert advice and for their help with editing.

To Brian Kerr, Manager of St Patrick's Athletic AFC, and to Jimmy Byrne of the Wheelchair Association and the Paralympics for all their help over the years.

To Liz Browne, Dave O'Neill, Andre and Evelyn Devereux, Ariel Townsend, Dr Brigid Sheehy, Lavina Collins, Dr Brian O'Shea, Kian Khatibi, Teenagh Cunningham, Dr John Godfrey Heathcote, Derek Jones, Marie-Elaine Grant, Bride Rosney, Aine Hearns, Eithne Barry, Alicia Berea-Gurielli, Dermot Clarke, Dr Bob Jones, John Treanor, Eric Guiry, Hilda O'Connell, Mairead Glynn, Sandra Conway and Eliza Kimball.

To Seamus Cashman, Susan Houlden, editor, Jenna Dowds and Ciara Considine whose patience and hard work made my life much easier across the miles.

To all my other colleagues and associates too numerous to mention on both sides of the Atlantic, especially my good friends in Bronxville, New York.

Foreword

The Japanese calligraphers and *Suiboku* (ink-painting) artists spend quite a long time producing a perfect tone of black for their artistic works. In fact, they grind the inkstick on the inkstone while they concentrate their minds before starting the real work. Once their brushes touch the paper or silk, they feel more or less as though their work is already completed. The well-known sword fighter of the 17th century, Miyamoto Musashi, was also a fine artist who produced many *Suiboku* painting under the name of Miyamoto Niten. After a lengthy period of concentration, he would start painting with strong and fast brush strokes as though he were using his sword in an actual fight.

In this book, the author expresses her extensive and remarkable knowledge of Oriental philosophy and culture. I have known her from the early days when she was teaching and studying at Sophia University in Tokyo. In those days she was a typical young Western psychologist, attempting to understand the Oriental way of thinking. Now, through her own personal experiences, she has attained her goal in a much more valuable way than she could ever have done through attending lectures or reading text books.

Above all, she has found the key to realising that composure of mind is of the greatest importance – not only for the performing artist or public figure but also for the sportsman. No matter how excellent or talented one may be, a peaceful state of mind is an essential element for true success.

Yoshiko Ushioda,
The Japanese Curator,
Chester Beatty Library

Part I

ZEN IN THE WAYS

This world
Is but
A fleeting dream
So why be alarmed
At its evanescence?

Ikkyu,
Three Zen Masters,
John Stevens,
Kodansha International (1993)

Chapter 1

The beginning of the journey

You are here to learn as well as to teach.
William Johnston SJ

As the Japan Air Lines 707 winged its way over the moonlit wastes of snow-covered Siberia one December night in 1975, descending at last in the harsh lights of Tokyo's Haneda airport, I was totally unaware of the effect some aspects of Japanese culture would have on my life, or how it would lead me into a new area of sports psychology. My husband Niall, an Irish diplomat, had been sent there three months previously, directly after our wedding, and I was a little apprehensive as to how I would react to my altered lifestyle as a diplomatic wife, having just given up my job as a clinical psychologist, running the psychology department in a Dublin teaching hospital.

Cherry blossom

The first few weeks passed in a daze, adjusting to the new sights and sounds of this exotic city and coping with the masses of people and endless streams of cars. I contrasted the small Georgian city of Dublin, banded by the sea on one side and the hills on the other, with the miles of concrete buildings of this huge metropolis. Niall showed me around with great enthusiasm: the Yasukuni Shrine which would soon be covered in spring cherry blossom, the moat surrounding the beautiful old palace of the Emperor, cosmopolitan Ginza and the sushi bars. We walked everywhere, exploring the city with great delight. I undertook an intensive course in Japanese so that I could travel around with ease as soon as possible. At that time very few people, even in Tokyo, spoke much English and it was necessary to have a basic knowledge of the language although unfortunately this was not adequate for more meaningful conversations. It was, however, particularly useful when, a few weeks later, I started lecturing at the University of Maryland, Far East Division, on the military bases outside Tokyo. It was on these long train journeys to the various bases in Yokosuka, Yokota, Zama and Yokohama that I learnt the art of sleeping – or at least being in a deep state of relaxation – while 'strap-hanging' for several hours, and as a result, arriving at my destination quite refreshed. The trains, I had noticed when I first arrived, were packed with apparently sleeping Japanese who would suddenly rise and alight at their correct station and it certainly didn't take me long to acquire this art.

Soon I also began to teach in the department of Comparative Culture on the Ichigaya campus at Sophia University, the Jesuit university in Tokyo, where many illustrious professors, including Heinrich Dumoulin and Enomiya Lassalle, were teaching. It was for me a unique experience as staff and students shared a common love of and interest in examining different aspects of East-West culture. Cross-cultural classes were the norm, where Chen, a blind Taiwanese acupuncturist, might share his experience with Wayne, an American ex-marine, or Margot, the wife of a German banker. These were classes in which learning was a many-directional process (unlike many Western universities in those days) and where ideas flowed freely – although often interrupted momentarily by shaking and rumbling as the old building moved, sometimes almost imperceptibly, sometimes strongly, with the frequent earthquakes.

Yeats and Joyce

Every month we would go to the Sacred Heart University for a meeting of the Japan-Ireland literature society. This was organised by a group of Japanese professors who had a special interest in Irish literature. We would gather around the long polished table listening to various discussions on comparisons between the work of Yeats and Joyce and Japanese writers. Sometimes Crown Princess Michiko – now the Empress of Japan – would join us at these meetings, exchanging the formality of the Imperial Palace for the relaxed surroundings of the college where once she had been a student. The elderly nuns who ran the college would talk with great affection of their most famous student, the pretty, lively girl who would one day be the Empress. On one occasion Sister Maher, who at this time was in her seventies, discussed her experiences during the Second World War. When a Japanese officer had come to intern her as a foreigner, she refused, saying she was Irish and Ireland was a neutral country. 'Ah yes,' said the officer, 'Ireland may be neutral – but it's neutral on the wrong side.'

Japanese culture

It was at this time that we became involved in many fascinating discussions with Professor William Johnston, the well-known Irish Jesuit who had lectured for many years at Sophia and who is one of the greatest authorities on Christian mysticism and Zen meditation. When he later suggested that I might assist with his graduate courses, I was pleased but initially somewhat nervous because I was well aware that the students were there primarily to listen to him. As I approached the classroom on the morning of the first day of the course William Johnston, noticing my anxiety, rebuked me sternly with the words 'You are here to learn as well as to teach', underlining the arrogance of the idea that to teach you have to know everything – thus creating anxiety as you concentrate on the impression you are making on others rather than on the task in hand. So for several years in Tokyo I learnt and I taught, but mostly I learnt and had never felt at any point in my life more fulfilled in my work. As nearly three short years passed, Niall and I studied Japanese culture and Christian Zen with William Johnston, Professor Kadawaki and other distinguished Jesuit and Japanese scholars. We travelled around Japan and the Far East. I read all I could including a very special book by Eugen Herrigel, a German philosophy professor, entitled *Zen in the Art of Archery*, which typifies for me the depth and beauty of the Japanese approach to life:

> For some considerable time it has been no secret, even to us Europeans, that the Japanese arts go back for their inner form to a common root, namely Buddhism. This is as true of the art of archery as of ink painting, of the art of the theatre no less than the tea ceremony, the art of flower arrangement and swordsmanship.[1]

Niall and I had many long interesting discussions with our Japanese and Western friends. We admired the depth and tranquility of the traditional ways based on Zen culture and we wondered how the materialistic vulgarity of the present day could co-exist with the dignified culture of old Japan, although in fact, it is as a result of Zen methods with their vitality, spontaneity and disciplined creativity that modern Japanese business practices have become a world force.

I meditated in meditation halls (*dojo*) and beside clear flowing streams, and I began to see and appreciate the transient beauty of the seasons so revered by the Japanese – the burning red Japanese maple leaves in autumn, the snow flakes in winter and the fleeting cherry blossom in spring.

> Ah, how glorious!
> Green leaves, young leaves
> Glittering in the sunlight

Bashō[2]

Zen ideal

One experience which summed up for me the Zen ideal remains firmly etched on my mind after all those years. This was a visit to an old Japanese house in Yokohama with Mrs Sato, a Japanese friend who had long shown an interest in young problem children who were involved with the family court. Removing our shoes, we went into a room where a group of young boys were kneeling on either side of a long low table. As we entered they all bowed low, greeting us politely yet cheerfully. Various stones of differing sizes lay in front of the boys, each of whom was polishing a stone with a soft cloth. These special stones, some no bigger than a fingernail, others the size of a big boulder, were originally of a very rough texture and after several weeks and months of polishing, the surface of each became like smooth black marble, exposing interesting fossil formations in the shape of a chrysanthemum (*kiku*).

After watching the boys polishing in a calm, disciplined manner, we drank some green Japanese tea (*cha*) with the couple, Mr and Mrs Hanawa, who ran the house, as they explained in their gentle way the purpose and outcome of their work during the previous seventeen years. The boys who had passed through

this house over the years had all experienced difficulties with
their parents and with society and would normally have been
placed in a remand home. Instead, they stayed in this unusual
setting for four to eight months, polishing these stones day
by day. Although they were producing beautiful works of art,
the purpose of their training was much more profound. It was
intended that through their work they might 'start to regain
affection for and trust in humanity, to learn persistence and
a disciplined endurance of the difficulties in life, in order to
develop into more mature and responsible personalities'.
Certainly the long-term results over the years had been encouraging and most of the boys had obtained employment and
found a respected place in society, important factors in every
culture but of particular importance in a formal traditional
culture such as Japan. There was, unlike so many other methods,
no stigma attached to anyone undergoing this form of treatment. The atmosphere in the home was rather one of mutual
care and understanding, very similar to that engendered in the
study of one of the Japanese traditional arts.

Boundless space

The time taken up with lecturing, treating patients and as a wife
involved in the hectic Tokyo diplomatic scene meant that I did
not have sufficient time to study – as formally as I would have
wished – these traditional arts in Japan. It was therefore wonderful to discover, on my return to Ireland, that I would be able to
study in greater detail the Japanese Tea Ceremony (*cha-no-u*)
with Iwasa Sensei[3], a highly respected master of the Tea Ceremony, who was living in Ireland for a few years. The tea-room
was an ordinary, small room in suburban Dublin but the material
surroundings weren't important the atmosphere was imbued
with the reverence and harmony of a traditional Japanese tea-
room, whose beauty Yasunari Kawabata, the 1968 Nobel laureate
for literature, described in his acceptance speech:

> The tea-room so rigidly confined and simple, contains
> boundless space and unlimited elegance. The single flower
> contains more brightness than a hundred flowers.[4]

Week after week and month after month, I and three Japanese
ladies learnt how to arrange the room for the tea ceremony, how

to prepare the tea utensils and how to carry them to and place them in the room. We then studied the roles of the various guests, how to formally accept and pass on the tea bowl and, finally, the difficult role of the host, how to prepare and serve the tea. As we knelt on our heels, our backs quite straight, carefully observing the actions of Iwasa Sensei, we were so aware that out of the apparently restricted discipline of these rituals come the spontaneity and dignified beauty, so obvious in the flowing movements of the master. This sitting position was maintained for long periods of time during our training, and at those times I experienced a whole range of emotional and physical responses, including feelings of boredom, pains in the knees and thighs and sometimes the loss of all sensation in my feet and lower limbs. Then at times, while in the background the gentle hiss of the kettle on the charcoal was barely audible, a deep feeling of tranquility and peace took over, the individual self was no longer a focus of primary awareness, there was harmony with the surroundings, nothing jarred. The relation-ship with the *sensei* was of great importance to us all on these occasions. She elicited from us feelings of deep respect and affection, as she gave everything of herself with a dignified and caring attitude, to guide us in the discipline of the Tea Cere-mony, which meant so much to her.

This relationship of guidance and mutual caring and respect without need for power or forced dependency is similar – as the great American psychologist Erich Fromm has pointed out – to a good relationship between psychotherapist and patient and also, as I later came to realise, to that between coach and athlete:

> It might be said that the Zen master loves his students. His love is one of realism and maturity, of making every effort to help the student in achieving his aim, and yet of know-ing that nothing the master does can solve the problem *for* the student, can achieve the aim for him.[5]

'Zone' or flow state

At this stage, I was keenly aware of how relevant this Zen philosophy was to therapeutic ideas and had been trying for some time to see how I could incorporate these ideas in the framework of my western psychotherapeutic training. The formulation of these ideas, I knew, was there somewhere, but I just could not work out how to use it in a meaningful way. The Japanese psychiatrist Tomio Hirai[6] had actually used some of these ideas over the years in his Zen meditation therapy and I was aware of this but maybe I was afraid at that time to try something too different in a western setting and needed to find some way to fit the ideas in with my own experience and western approach. Ironically, the solution finally came from an area other than therapy. It was 1979, the year before the Moscow Olympics, and my first problem at the Dublin hospital where I had started to work was introduced by Tom Shakespeare, the archery coach for the Irish Olympic team. Tom was very aware, even at that time, of the role of psychology in sport and he introduced to me one team member who was under-performing because of poor motivation and concentration. The coach described the state of mind conducive to skilful shooting – a state whereby internal and external distractions were not attended to, whereby everything flowed, temporal and spatial dimensions were altered and the target couldn't be missed – called the 'flow state'[7] or 'zone' in archery. As he spoke I realised that this state of mind was similar to that obtained in Zen meditation and knew that here at last was a way to start incorporating these ideas into my work. The major problem of this 'zone' was that individuals never knew when or how they could attain the state and, as soon as they thought about it, they lost it. If there was, therefore, a way in which archers could learn to induce this state at will and bring it more under their control, the opportunities for superior shooting would become more frequent. One way might be by training them to achieve a similar distractionless state – i.e. Zen meditation in general life – which then could be transferred to archery practice and competition. The archers read and enjoyed Herrigel's book, but it did not mean much to them at that time as they wanted a more practical programme.

Induce the 'zone'

Over the next eight months I developed a programme using Zen meditation, psychotherapy and relaxation techniques to try to train Phil Egan, the first archer involved in the programme, to induce this 'zone' at will and be able to bring his mental state more under control. Phil was a very talented archer, ranked fifth or sixth in the Irish team, who had not been progressing as fast as he should, and had even been considering giving up archery. Consequently he participated with great enthusiasm in the programme, very soon showing great improvement and he was able to induce the 'zone' much more frequently than before. At the trials to select Olympic competitors, he beat the others by a very large margin. His progress had been unusually rapid, but despite this, Phil was not chosen to go to Moscow, which set the programme back quite a lot. It was still, I suppose, early days for this sort of thinking in Irish sport. I did however, continue to see some other archers, including Richard Delaney, the Irish crossbow champion for many years. He was a gentle, charming man, who worked hard on his mental programme and also showed some good results at that time.

Stress reduction

I was just starting to change the programme into one which would involve treating the stress symptoms of patients suffering from coronary disease, when in 1981 Niall was transferred as Chargé d'Affaires to the Irish embassy in Iran. This involved a period of more adjustment, especially in a country in the throes of recent revolution and at war with neighbouring Iraq. Although the back page of the *Tehran Times* proclaimed boldly each day that 'Archery and swimming are sports of the prophet', there was at that time very little outlet for sport, except diplomatic tennis courts, swimming pools and 'his' and 'her' skiing slopes. These segregated slopes were patrolled by revolutionary guards (*pasdars*) checking whether or not skiing outfits were sufficiently Islamic – hardly a forum for serious sports.

I was, however, soon involved in treating foreigners and westernised Iranians who were suffering from stress problems; I adapted my programme for this purpose. I was also myself able to approach therapy from a different point of view as the whole experience was quite stressful for me. We had a constant police guard on the embassy, where we lived, and were dealing with the continual threat of violence and Iraqi air raids, not to mention harassment by the *pasdars* to cover every inch of flesh and

strand of hair. I could therefore understand only too well the
pressure everyone was under and found it an interesting and
challenging and at times frightening situation, so different from
the usual therapeutic procedure I was accustomed to. As soon
as I arrived I went to the German Institute where all the psychology
journals were kept, but found that they stopped at the beginning
of the revolution, in October 1978. Maybe in retrospect this
proved to be a positive set of circumstances, as I then began
again to study the old Japanese ideas and Sufi writings.

Sufism

As a release from the pressure of revolutionary violence and
food shortages, I began to study calligraphy with an old Sufi
master, Ustad Abdolrasouli, one of the most famous calligraphers and traditional musicians of his time, descended from a
long line of famous philosophers and mullahs. He had carried
out the calligraphy adorning the famous shrine of Omar Khyam,
Sufi poet and astrologer, at Nishapur in the north of Iran. He
spent his days writing verses of the Koran in the most exquisite
Persian calligraphy and also copying lines from Hafez – probably the most revered Persian poet – and the *Rubaiyat* of Omar
Khayyam, along with other Sufi poets.

> The worldly hope men set their hearts upon
> Turns ashes – or it prospers; and anon,
> Like snow upon the desert's dusty face
> Lighting a little hour or two – is gone.

Omar Khayyam

Sufism, being the mystical part of Islam, is close in so many ways
to Zen and Christian mysticism, stressing as it does the need for
pure experience of the Truth rather than verbal descriptions.
The house of Ustad Abdolrasouli was for us a haven of peace in
the turmoil of life in Teheran and encapsulated much of our
Japanese cultural experience. It was a place filled with culture
and creativity, where traditional musicians and writers gathered to discuss ideas. It was here that one of his pupils started
to teach me the Persian setar – a four-stringed traditional
musical instrument – and, by studying in a minor way these
Persian arts and translations of the great Sufi poets, maybe I
came a little closer to understanding the Persian psyche.

I left Iran at the end of 1986 and again started my programme for stress and sport just a few months prior to the 1988 Seoul Olympics.

Under-performance in sport

The results in sport were very interesting, although these were relative of course to each athlete's performance rather than to international standards. In 1989 I was appointed as psychologist to the Olympic Council of Ireland's medical committee for the Barcelona Olympic Games. The major question here that I had to answer was would these ideas work equally well for all sports or were they specific solely to archery. I felt that they probably would be relevant to all sports. The central issue in any sport was, I believed, under-performance, due to lack of concentration and an inability to cope with competition stress. OCI President Pat Hickey, a judo player, and therefore well versed in Eastern techniques and supportive of my ideas, asked me to conduct a pilot study on the judo team. One individual, although very talented, had not won any competition outside Ireland for several years because of his inability to cope with psychological stress. After three sessions, however, he won a bronze medal at an international event, reinforcing the feeling that at least we seemed to be on the right track. Even ten years after I first started, although sports psychology was now accepted all over the world, it was still difficult to convince many people in Irish sport of the need for such techniques. It was probably more difficult due to the fact that I was using an Eastern theme. Fortunately, there were enough good results to encourage me to continue despite a less than enthusiastic response from some quarters.

World rowing champion

These techniques do not of course work for every individual since and not everyone can use them with the necessary open-minded disciplined approach. One who did, however, was Niall O'Toole, the highly talented young rower who surprised many by winning the 1991 World Lightweight rowing championship at the age of twenty-one. He found that with them he could cope with distractions and psychological stress more easily and within months he climbed from sixth in the world to world champion as he learnt how to channel all his energy into his performance – thus proving his natural ability as well as his coach Michael Desmond's expertise. He found that after several weeks he was able to put himself into the 'zone' at will, get extremely fast starts and feel much more in control. Good results have also been achieved in many other areas of sport, including golf, tennis, boxing, athletics and swimming and those athletes who use the techniques correctly have shown great improvement.

That same year the Irish boxing team, under the guidance of Nicholas Cruz, the Cuban coach, started to use the techniques in preparation for the European championships in Sweden. The whole team performed very well, especially Paul Griffin who returned home with the first European gold medal for forty-two years. At the time Paul hadn't been too sure of the value of these techniques but later he explained how he had used them and how they had helped him.

Creativity

I had also started to use these techniques in the area of creativity – looking at individual ability to harness the 'zone' for activities such as writing, art and music. My personal experience was very useful here too. Although over the years I had of course been using Zen meditation myself and had been closely involved with the ideas in my work and lifestyle, I had not used the techniques in any specific way related to a plan of action – as had the athletes. I started to do so as the result of an unusual set of adventures.

Invasion

On 2 August 1990, the Iraqis moved into Kuwait and two weeks later, when every sensible person, including most diplomats, was trying to leave Baghdad and Kuwait, my husband Niall was sent to Amman and the following week flew into Baghdad. Within days of the invasion, almost all flights had stopped, commercial links had been broken and the television screens were filled with harrowing pictures of refugees streaming across the desert to the Jordanian border where they were being housed in makeshift camps. Then the news broke of diplomatic immunity being withdrawn in Kuwait for diplomats who refused to leave. Threats and counter-threats filled those uncertain days as Saddam Hussein preached destruction on one side and President Bush took to the golf course in a pose of strained normality while American and European troops were preparing for war. Western men left behind in Kuwait had gone into hiding as otherwise they would be used as 'human shields' and detained at strategic military centres which were liable to be attacked. It was at that time that I settled down to write the report on my initial pilot study for the Olympic Council of Ireland. For two weeks I sat before an empty sheet of paper, my mind filled with distractions and uncertainty as I worried about the effect of this on Clare and Andrew, our two young children, who were only six and four years old at the time. On the occasions when he could get through on the telephone from Baghdad, Niall would say that everything was fine, although this did not fit in with the daily news on the media and the desperate pleas of families whose relatives were hostages.

Harness energy

Finally I decided to use the meditation specifically to calm my mind and to gather my distracted energy into my ideas. I found my mind clearing and becoming more focused as I centred my thoughts on the rhythm of my breathing. Focused, I picked up my pen and, eager to start writing, wrote five or six foolscap pages – the content had never been a problem but harnessing my energy certainly was. From then on I had no trouble working at that difficult time, which was just as well, because several weeks later I lost all contact with Niall for a week. I was only afterwards informed that he had gone to Kuwait to contact Irish citizens in hiding there and had been arrested by Iraqi troops, who had burst into the Canadian embassy where he and some other foreign diplomats were arranging an escape flight for women and children out of Kuwait. The diplomats as well as six Irish hostages (male civilians who had been in hiding) were taken away to a military detention camp. Fortunately, they were all released after several hours and the six Irish civilians were allowed to leave with my husband for Baghdad.

Severalweeks later they were transferred safely to Ireland. This specific incident led, among other things, to the adoption of Resolution 667 by the United Nations Security Council – but for me it was a time when I learnt more about myself and my work. From then on I rarely write anything without using these techniques. I sit at my desk overlooking Dublin Bay, dispel my distracting thoughts and gather my energy, slowly breathing, one with the rhythm of the waves, losing myself in the gentle ebb and flow of the grey-green sea. Now I feel more in control of any creative work I might undertake.

Barcelona Olympic Games

In 1992 I went as the official psychologist with the Irish team to the Barcelona Olympic Games. It was the first time a psychologist had been appointed to travel with the squad and, sadly, most of the team were still very wary about the benefits of sports psychology. Not all the athletes, therefore, were willing to consult me. One of the principal groups with which I did work, however, was again the boxing team. Foremost in this group were three men: the Dublin coach, Austin Carruth, with whom I had liaised closely for some years; Nicholas Cruz, the Cuban coach who appreciated the role of psychologists from his experiences with the Cuban teams; and team manager Sean Horkan whose calm manner helped to hold the team together.

The boxing world had over the previous couple of years been surprisingly open to new influences, as other sports psychologists in Barcelona confirmed. As a team, we had engaged in many discussions at training camps in Drogheda and now in the hot sun of the Olympic Village, we had individual and group discussions. I watched the training sessions, checking that they included the concentration techniques and occasionally being splashed with water amid howls of laughter, as they combined their sense of fun with disciplined training. 'Breathe, Felicity,' they would shout when consternation passed over my face – quite a frequent occurrence.

Most of the boxing team performed well at Barcelona. Paul Douglas was injured at the beginning of his contest for the bronze medal, but he had already beaten two world-ranked boxers in two excellent fights. Two boxers achieved medals,

Michael Carruth won gold and Wayne McCullough won silver. Michael's gold medal was the first Olympic gold in Irish sport since 1956 when Ronnie Delaney, coached by Jumbo Elliott, won the 1500 metres in Melbourne.

Jigsaw puzzle

The whole point of the Zen programme is that it helps the athlete to fulfil his potential by controlling that elusive factor, the mind. The psychological factor had been missing in Irish sport over the years, especially when compared to other countries. The mental training area is only a small piece of the jigsaw puzzle but, if it is missing, the picture can never be complete. Maybe this time all the pieces of the jigsaw had finally been slotted together.

Paralympics

In February 1992, I also started to work with Jimmy Byrne of the Irish Wheelchair Association and those members of his association who were to participate in the Paralympics to be held in Barcelona the following September. This was an excellent experience for me because almost every member of the team was aware of the importance of a strong psychological input as part of their preparation and all responded very positively. The good results in Barcelona were not necessarily proven by the award of medals but by the fact that almost all those competing achieved a personal best. In view of this they and their coaches were delighted.

Tune in to the 'zone'

The results of this approach were very interesting in all areas, including psychological and physical disorders, business stress and musical and artistic performance. Any area, in fact, where an alert concentrated state of mind and calm relaxed approach helps the individual to produce a fully rounded performance and see events from a different, less emotional, point of view. Many individuals were able to 'tune in' to the 'zone' – although previously this had not been possible for them. They were able to acknowledge that only in this state could they perform to the best of their ability.

I had started (after the Moscow Olympics) to write some articles about this work with the original teams, although not without trepidation, as Zen encourages experience and training, rather than verbalisation. It was only after I had worked with more groups and teams, however, that I could test these theories more comprehensively. The results are showing how useful Zen principles can be in sport and other areas and I have now put these ideas together in a way which I hope will be of benefit to others in all walks of life.

One day in the summer of 1978, as I was walking out of Sophia University with William Johnston into the narrow sunlit streets of Ichigaya, discussing the progress of his new book on mysticism, he turned to me and remarked: 'You write a book when you have something to say.'

Now, many years later, I feel that I do have something that should be said.

Chapter 2

The martial arts

It is easiest to have a first experience-flash of Zen realization in some Way like flower arrangement, in a static environment, but the combative arts are capable of a clearer expression of Zen because they require immediate response in a potentially serious situation. It is true that today they are mainly practised as sports, but the tension at time of contest is sometimes as great as at times of real danger.[1]

China had already been influenced by Buddhist philosophy for several centuries when an Indian monk, Bodhidharma (the twenty-eighth Indian Patriarch and first Chinese Zen Patriarch), is believed to have arrived in the south of the country in about the early sixth century AD. It was he, above all, who is traditionally held to be responsible for the merging of Indian thought with the Taoist and other Chinese philosophies prevalent there at the time and became the founder of Zen in China. Zen is the Japanese pronunciation of the Chinese ch'an – derived originally from the Sanskrit *dhyana* – and may be translated as meditation or contemplation. In the twelfth century Zen was brought from China to Japan by Eisai and Dogen and became the basis of so much creative, spiritual and cultural expression in Japan. Of the main schools of Zen in Japan, the Rinzai school invokes the use of the *koan*, a riddle which has no logical answer, to bring about enlightenment. The Soto school established by Dogen also makes some use of the *koan* but mainly places emphasis on *zazen* (sitting meditation).

But what exactly is Zen?
This is an extremely difficult question as Zen is full of paradoxes and its apparent simplicity defies ready definition.

> Not thinking about anything is Zen. Once you know this,
> standing, walking, sitting or lying down, everything you
> do is Zen.[2]

An adequate description of the essence of Zen is verbally impossible and that is why wordless transmission 'from heart to
heart' has been emphasised over the centuries. This is perhaps
best illustrated by the occasion when the Buddha Shakyamuni
is said to have held up a flower to a large assembly and his main
disciple Kasyapa smiled – for he alone understood. As Heinrich
Dumoulin expresses it:

> A deep silence hovers over the occurrence; not a word is
> spoken. The Buddha holds up the flower, the disciple
> smiles. Thus is Zen. Because supreme truth cannot be
> spoken in words, there has to be a wordless transmission
> outside the scriptures.[3]

So too in Taoism, from which so much of Zen thought springs,
the emphasis is on non-verbal teaching and as Lao-tzu affirmed
so long ago, in the *Tao Te Ching*, this cannot be expressed
verbally:

> Those who know do not speak;
> Those who speak do not know.

Ordinary mind

Zen is often referred to as 'ordinary mind', nothing special, nothing
unusual, no ecstasy, just a complete pure condition. It is in fact that
very normal condition that our desires and needs destroy. The
masters teach us to experience life fully and simply and pay no
heed to the incessant chatter of our supposedly sophisticated
minds. As the Zen master Rinzai said: 'When hungry, I eat; when
tired, I sleep. Fools laugh at me. The wise understand.'[4]

We should live life in the present, every moment experienced
as our last – for that moment is all we have, that exact moment
will never return. Zen has to be experienced, not discussed; for
if we only talk about things we can never truly 'know' them. This
is similar to other forms of mysticism – although many students
of Zen would be inclined not to label Zen as such. The medieval
Christian mystic, Meister Eckhart, puts it another way:

> The shell must be cracked apart if what is in it is to come
> out, for if you want the kernel you must break the shell.[5]

William Johnston, writing about the author of *The Cloud of Unknowing*, the anonymous fourteenth-century English mystic, gave the following advice:

> When you go apart to be alone for prayer, put from your mind everything you have been doing or plan to do. Reject all thoughts, be they good or be they evil.

Johnston goes on to say about the mystic that 'in his rejection of conceptualisation, he is as radical as any Zen Buddhist.[6]

In Islamic mysticism, the Sufi poets also employ the concept that the Ultimate Truth is hidden and must be unveiled to be 'known':

> O lift thy veil to me,
> When I thy glory see:
> Then shall I rend apart
> The garments of my heart.[7]

Perhaps this is best illustrated by a fascinating Sufi twelfth century fable composed by Farid ud-Din Attar. The story relates an allegorical journey towards self-enlightenment and union with God, a journey beset – as would be any such endeavour – by apparently insurmountable obstacles. A group of birds set out to find the *Simurgh*, the ruler of all birds and the source of Being. Most gave up the search in the course of the journey but, by detaching themselves from the material world, thirty birds found at last what they sought. Finally in the presence of the *Simurgh*, they asked for an explanation of the ineffable secrets of the universe. The *Simurgh* wordlessly replied:

> The sun of my majesty is a mirror. He who sees himself therein sees his soul and his body, and sees them completely. Since you have come as thirty birds, *si-murgh*, you will see thirty birds in this mirror.[8]

The birds learned at the end of their difficult travels the meaning of the unity of the universe but – as in the Taoist and Zen texts – discovered it could not be explained verbally but only by direct experience and non-verbal transmission.

Being not judging

In Zen, use is made of the symbolism of a mind being like a mirror – not attached, not clinging to its image. It accepts the reflection without judgment or prejudice and then lets go, leaving no trace – this is perhaps one of the most difficult tasks for all of us – not to judge, not to prejudge, not to cling to reasons and motives for action, just to let go and to be. This of course does not mean acting carelessly and without thought or compassion. It actually means the very opposite; it means living more conscientiously by forgetting thoughts of gain and glory and concentrating on the task in hand. In terms of Western sport it means not worrying about prizes or medals but training day after day so that on the day of competition you will be able to do your very best to fulfil your potential to function fully, not distracted or fearful, arrogant or careless. This means 'learning to concentrate all one's energies and faculties on one thing at a time and yet remain aware of everything else that is going on around one'.[9] In other words, one must live life fully in regard to everything, single-mindedly concentrating on the task in hand yet relaxed.

Are the Ways too complex for the West?

Some years ago, the Ways were perhaps the only method permitted to non-Japanese, as Herrigel found when, anxious to study Zen, he was advised instead to study one of the martial arts; he chose archery (*kyudo*).

Jung echoed the views of most Japanese scholars by suggesting that Zen was not suitable for Westerners in general; their minds, he felt, were not sufficiently disciplined to cope with the rigours of Zen training.[10] Perhaps to an extent he was right or at least not totally wrong – for study both of Zen and the Ways – because whereas these Ways are highly regarded in Japan, most Westerners often regard them as merely sports and artistic pursuits. In the East on the other hand they are regarded more as a path leading to spiritual development, or as a way to perfection – a state where the goal is secondary to the mental discipline and to the attainment of a selfless state of harmony.

Technique – wasa

Many people might assume at this stage that in such circumstances the achievement of the technique is not too important. This of course is not so; technique is obviously essential in all martial arts and activities, it is necessary to learn the various skills and to practise and practise until all this becomes second nature. At this stage the techniques and methods are forgotten; the individual lost in perfect concentration can transcend his training.

Just as in Western sport, a good mental approach is not enough if sufficient training has not been undertaken. So even if adequate training is undertaken, without the spiritual aspect the action becomes lifeless, inspiration becomes mere mechanical technical ability, lacking in creativity and spontaneity. This state is detected immediately in the work or performance by the experienced, practised eye, but maybe is not discernible to the uninitiated.

Transient vitality and beauty

When I was studying Persian calligraphy, the Sufi master could immediately tell when I was in a creative state of mind by the flow and balance of my writing: a state of mind full of life and vigour yet paradoxically empty – unaware of the self. I wasn't sure that I could tell too much myself, but I would know by the way everything felt 'right', no trying, no straining, just 'effortless' effort. After months and years of my copying lines and curves of his graceful Persian script, on rare occasions would he declare that I had attained success. For a brief period the *imitation process* had become *spontaneous* and *creative*, and the writing had begun to take on a transient vitality and beauty of its own.

No direct instruction in the Ways

Many proponents of the martial arts point out that is no concentration on progression in the Ways; in fact there is rarely any instruction given in the Ways themselves, maybe because it is not possible to give direct instruction in attaining the depth and tranquility of self-transcendence. Initially the practise of the techniques and methods is all-important and must be undertaken with total dedication. The pupil does not appear to be allowed free expression but must follow the example of the master meticulously, even down to what appears to be the most tedious detail.

Martial arts — Budo

In heaven and earth, no chink to hide,
Joy to know the man is void and the things too are void,
Splendid the great Mongolian long sword,
Its lightning flash cuts the spring breeze.[11]

When ki fills the body

It is in the martial arts that the truest expression of Zen is found, particularly in bygone eras when a lapse in concentration could mean instant death. This was a time when a fearless alert readiness of mind and body was not just preferable for well-being but was essential for survival. More than that, however, was the ultimate perfection, the overcoming of the fear of death. A recent Japanese ambassador to Ireland, Yuzo Hatano, was from a family well versed in the Ways. His father was a calligrapher and famous Noh actor who had been given the title 'Living Treasure' – the highest accolade that can be awarded to any artist or cultural figure in Japan. In his old age he had been sick for some time and one day, in the tradition of many of the old masters, he said to those around his bed, 'Thank you everybody, today I want to be excused,' and died. The ambassador told me how, when he was studying the martial arts, he prepared himself at the start of a competition: 'I meditated and composed myself for several seconds until I felt ready'. I inquired at what point did he realise he was ready and he answered: 'When I sensed that *ki* filled my body.'

It is difficult to find an adequate translation for *ki*; this sense of universal energy or life-force is, however, a central concept in the martial arts. The seat of energy is the *hara*, the lower abdominal area. It is when the body feels strong and stable, in harmony with itself and free from distracting thoughts that intuitively one is ready for action. An important concept here is *mushin* – no mind, where thoughts come and go but no thoughts cling, like a mirror or still water reflecting and letting go:

With no mind, blossoms invite the butterfly;
With no mind, the butterfly visits the blossoms,
When the flower blooms, the butterfly comes;
When the butterfly comes, the flower blooms.
I do not 'know' others,

Others do not 'know' me.
Not-knowing each other we naturally follow the Way.

Ryokan[12]

The mind is uncalculating, free, flowing, detached, not worry-ing, analysing, self-seeking or clinging to distractions. This is also similar to the state of *samadhi*[13] which is an essential mental component of successful martial arts. It is too late when engaged in combat to start working out one's own strategy or that of the opponent, there is no time to worry about previous mistakes or to think of one's own prowess. Thought and action have to be simultaneous or the consequences could be deadly. At that point time, space and thought stand still in action.

Blocked energy

When we are not trying desperately to achieve something, often everything works out of its own accord and we attain success; when, however, our minds and bodies are not at one – when they are straining, striving, clinging to distractions – then our physical and psychic energy is blocked and frustrated and we frequently wonder why we are not making adequate progress.

One story which illustrates this quandry is told by Lieh-Tzu, who talks of a young man who went alone each day to the beach where the sea-gulls and all the birds would come up to him. One day his father asked him to bring some birds back to him but the following morning the sea-gulls danced above the young man and would not come down. He had gone to the sea-shore with a purpose and that had prevented him from achieving what he most wanted. Previously he had allowed him just to be there with the birds and they had spontaneously come to him.[14]

Sometimes when athletes have not performed so well in com-petition they say: 'My rival wanted to win more than I did.' Further analysis often suggests, however, that they themselves have been concentrating too much on winning and at the time of the competition their energy has in fact been blocked by these covert needs; as a result, lethargy has crept in, dulling their performance.

Kendo

> Your Honour is indeed well versed in the art of the spear.
> But until you have known the state of wielding the spear
> with hands empty, you will not penetrate to the ultimate
> secret of the art.[15]

Kendo, the Way of the sword, came to the fore during the
Tokugawa era, a relatively peaceful time in Japan when the
warrior clans had been disbanded and those who were not
retained by the Shoguns became ronin (wandering warriors).
Miyamoto Mushashi was one of these ronin and he became one
of the most accomplished swordsmen of all centuries, but even
after he was accepted as such in his own lifetime he continued
to practise, searching for ultimate perfection.

Flexibility

Musashi advocates total flexibility in training, learning to deal
with all situations so that nothing is left to chance.

> You should not have a favourite weapon. To become over-
> familiar with one weapon is as much a fault as not knowing
> it sufficiently well.[16]

This is not perhaps applicable to all sports but it is certainly
important not to become too reliant on one piece of equipment
which – if it breaks prior to an important competition – can
create a problem of crisis proportions for the athlete. A variation
on this is the superstitious rituals which are commonly employed
by some athletes: if a favoured sequence is blocked or a special
object is lost, then performance can be badly affected.

Musashi furthermore points out that:

> Anyway if you learn indoor techniques, you will think
> narrowly and forget the true Way. Then you will have
> difficulties in actual encounters.[17]

Several competitors I have advised over the years have thought
that training in itself was sufficient in order to reach the pinnacle
of their sport. For various reasons they avoided competitions but
unfortunately discovered too late that 'actual encounters' (i.e.
testing oneself out under stress) are a necessary and important
stage in attaining success.

Rhythm and timing

One of Musashi's precepts is that 'there is timing in everything'.
He explains in detail how important is the concept of timing,
sensing this special time, acting and reacting neither too early
nor too late. 'Timing and rhythm are also involved in the military arts, shooting, bow and guns, and riding horses. In all skills
and abilities there is timing.'[18]

In *kendo* there is no time to make a decision as to what technique
would be best, no time to hesitate and analyse the weak points
of the opponent – 'intuition and action must spring forth at the
same time as Deshimaru illustrates:

> One day a samurai, a great master of the sword (*kendo*), set
> out to seek the secret of swordfighting. This was in the
> Tokugawa period. At midnight he went to the sanctuary
> at Kamakura, mounted the long flights of steps leading up
> to it, and did homage to the god of the place, Hachiman.
> In Japan Hachiman is a great *bodhisattva* who has become
> the patron of Budo. The samurai made his obeisance.
> Coming back down the steps he sensed, lurking under a
> big tree, the presence of a monster, facing him. Intuitively
> he drew his sword and slew it in the instant; the blood
> poured out and ran along the ground. He had killed it
> unconsciously.
>
> The *bodhisattva* Hachiman had not told him the secret of
> Budo, but because of this experience on his way back from
> the sanctuary, the samurai understood it.[19]

The individual must be relaxed yet concentrated, entirely
aware with all his senses of everything around him yet attending to nothing, clinging to nothing, neither thought nor
sound, aware of any movement of the sword, yet not distracted by it. One split second of indecision, one momentary
look of doubt in the eyes could be detected by the opponent.
It is obviously very difficult to maintain constant concentration
throughout the contest but one way to attempt to do this is to
focus all the time on your breathing – especially the exhalations
which should reach down into the abdomen, the *hara*, harnessing *ki* the energy of the universe, 'breathing from the heels' as
Chuang Tzu recommended.

There are stories of *kendo* masters facing each other unmoving, unflinching, both equally stable, *ki* balanced, until the contest is declared a draw. Other less experienced martial artists, feeling agitated would probably be forced into a premature attack. The ultimate in the martial arts is not to use the sword; having achieved perfection of mind the warrior is thus released from the fear of death.

Sense their feeling

In this context, a modern application was referred to in an interesting discussion I had one day with John Twomey, the Irish fencing champion, who had been training in Estonia. He remarked how coaches from many countries had trained him in technique, but his Estonian coach told him only to watch the best fencers as he was training, to sense their feeling, imitate them, be like them, not to concentrate so much on technique, but on that 'feeling', the special spirit of perfect fencing.

A passage from the Hagakure of the seventeenth century describes how those who have perfected the mind are immediately recognisable to masters of the martial arts as though they had already perfected those arts. During the Shogunate of Tokugawa, one of the guards of the Shoguns came to a famous *kendo* master for lessons in fencing. The master was sure that the pupil was already a trained swordsman but the pupil denied that. Finally the puzzle was solved when he admitted that for some years he had tried to come to terms with the problem of fear of death as a samurai and that finally death no longer worried him. It was this mastery that had been picked up by the *kendo* master – 'for the ultimate secrets of swordsmanship also lie in being released from the thought of death'.[20]

Karate-do

> The ultimate aim of the art of Karate lies not in the victory
> or defeat, but in the perfection of the character of its
> participants.[21]

Karate was brought to the islands of Okinawa from China where it had initially been developed around the sixth century AD as a form of unarmed combat. This form of combat was later divided into various forms of judo and karate and introduced to the Japanese mainland by Gichin Funakoshi, who said: 'Never forget the old saying that a strong wind may destroy a sturdy tree but the willow bows and the wind passes through. The great virtues of karate are prudence and humility'. [22]

Personal struggle

C W Nicol, who spent several years in Japan learning karate, describes his training with the Makiwara, the training post: 'It was (and still is) a deeply personal fight, nobody could watch me, see my little victories and defeats.'[23]

Maybe in this is the essence of all success whether in training or competition – that in the final analysis the supreme struggle is with oneself. Everyone else may be fooled but you alone know whether or not you are worthy of your victory and whether your achievement has been truly successful. Nicol learned to focus and compose his mind in training and found that punching the target became 'an exercise of concentration and release, it had rhythm, and the gradual building of awareness in timing, distance and strength'.[24] The techniques must be mastered by long hours of practise, a prerequisite before the power of the mind takes over, relaxed, flowing, transcendent of self and technique. However, as George Leonard describes, referring to his training in *aikido*, there is no easy answer, no quick method, no slick trick of technique:

> I recalled moments of grace, certain throws that seemed to build and break as if in rhythm with an ocean wave, revealing the inner perfection of all movement, all existence. But I could bring to mind no forced external 'perfection' based entirely on technique.[25]

The art of perfection is an ongoing process and as such is neverending – a point frequently acknowledged by Zen masters when asked how long should the practice of Zen be continued.

Single-minded

The importance of being single-minded is also emphasised by Nicol; when he tried initially to study both judo and karate at the one time, he was given the following advice: 'A hunter who chases two rabbits at the same time will catch neither of them.'[26]

It is essential to concentrate on whatever we do so that our energy is powerfully focused not directed into diverse actions. No one who wished to become a proficient golfer would seriously think of beginning tennis and golf lessons together. Only when we are accomplished in one area, can we gain fresh insight by taking up another similar pursuit.

The True Way

There are many stories of astounding feats by masters in karate and the other martial arts. The true master, however, never concentrates on such amazing events – as 'showmanship' of any nature is not the 'True Way'. They do not need to appear different or special or capable of 'super-human' activities. Lieh-tzu, indeed, warns us of attaining any form of honoured treatment, the 'empty' man does not attract attention. On one journey he returned soon after his departure because 'I ate at ten inns, and at five they served me first'. He was alarmed at this because 'when a man's inner integrity is not firm, something oozes from his body and becomes an aura, which outside him presses on the hearts of others; it makes other men honour him more than his elders and betters and gets him into difficulties'.[27]

Dignity and humility

In the martial arts, emphasis is placed on dignity and humility. A major negative factor in competitive sports, is that of concentrating on one's opponent or fellow-competitors to the detriment of one's own performance. It is essential to keep in mind that one's main rival is oneself. We can only improve by testing ourselves against fellow-competitors and they should accordingly be regarded as a challenge, not a threat. In the martial arts, the act of bowing low at various points in the course of a contest demonstrates respect for one's opponent, the laying down of the self. The training area or *dojo* is, as Joe Hyams suggests:

> An arena of confined conflict where we confront an opponent who is not an opponent but rather a partner engaged in helping us understand ourselves more fully.[28]

Baseball player Sadaharu Oh develops this point from his own experience:

In combat I learned to give up combat. I learned in fact that there were no enemies. An opponent was someone whose strength joined to yours created a certain result. Let someone call you an enemy and attack you and in that moment they lost the contest.[29]

On the whole, unfortunately, this idea is a fairly alien concept in Western sport, yet one from which we could gain much in all areas of life. The true champion knows he can be successful; he is quietly assured that his performance will be the best he is capable of achieving. The insecure champion, on the other hand, is often surprised when he performs to a high standard which he – and others – may attribute to a freak occurrence. Accordingly, he may brag and strut around in an attempt to convince himself, as much as others, of his prowess.

The Way of the bow – Kyudo

The spider dances her web without knowing that there are flies who will get caught in it. The fly, dancing nonchalantly on a sunbeam, gets caught in the net without knowing what lies in store. But through both of them 'It' dances, and inside and outside are united in this dance. So, too, the archer hits the target without having aimed.[30]

Right mind not tricks

So in Japanese archery the Way is again of essential significance. *Kyudo*, like *kendo*, is regarded as one of the most 'noble' arts. Herrigel describes evocatively his long, arduous journey searching for perfection of mind as well as technique. The frustration of the Western mind grappling with Eastern thought is excellently catalogued here. In lesson after lesson he attempted to fathom the 'trick' of perfect shooting; unfortunately these attempts only held him back as he analysed and agonised over his lack of progress. He falls into the all too familiar trap of so many athletes – trying too hard, straining and striving for perfection, the mind's tranquility clouded by that very effort as the muscles tense and energy is dissipated.

Eventually Herrigel learned to lose himself in his breathing so that his effort became effortless. Sometimes this happened so effectively that he felt that he himself was not breathing but 'being breathed'. When correct breathing has been accomplished and thoughts of shooting are eliminated, then the arrow is released like snow sliding naturally off a branch.

This is not really a reflex action because in martial arts it is not a mindless automatic process. It is rather a perfect state of awareness perfectly executed – decision-making processes always taken into account – as in the 'flow state' or 'zone' in sport.

Hara

The *hara* is a vital concept in all of the martial arts. Emphasis is placed on pushing the breath down into the lower abdomen and holding it before exhaling. I personally do not recommend either attempting to control the breathing by deliberately slowing it down or holding it; in some people, this might cause physical problems such as dizziness or uncomfortable chest pressure. This was confirmed for me in discussion with William Johnston and in Katsuki Sekida's book.[31] I have found that a means of achieving the desired effect is to breathe out gently through the nostrils, concentrating at the same time on the internal movement caused by the apparent pushing down of the breath into the region of the *hara*. Some athletes had difficulty with this concept initially but those who have successfully mastered this form of breathing, including boxer Michael Carruth, have found that it helps to produce a very composed and concentrated state of mind and more physical stability.

Mushin

The power of shooting should come from the stomach, without thought of gain or success, unconcerned at losing or performing or about how we might appear to others – a state of *mushin*. This may be illustrated by a story of Lieh-Tzu: When Yang Chu was passing through Sung he spent the night at an inn. The inn-keeper had two concubines, one beautiful and the other ugly. The ugly one he valued, the beautiful one he neglected. When Yang Chu asked the reason, the fellow answered:

> The beautiful one thinks herself beautiful, and I do not notice her beauty. The ugly one thinks herself ugly, and I do not notice her ugliness.

'Remember this, my disciples,' said Yang Chu. 'If you act nobly and banish from your mind the thought that you are noble, where can you go and not be loved?'[32]

Just as Lieh-Tzu tells us that a beautiful woman who is aware of her beauty becomes no longer attractive, so the archer who is focusing on his talent and whose thoughts are of how others see him is no longer able to perform perfectly:

An archer who acts from out of his 'full emptiness' functions with undivided perception, and will hit the target without fail despite not giving the least thought to that.[33]

Quieting the Mind

Some essential elements for successful study of the martial arts have been outlined in this chapter. Untiring dedication to training, quieting of the mind and the letting go of any interest in gain or loss – all these help to lead to 'perfection of action'. As Yagyu Munenori (1571-1646) suggested: 'Forgetting learning, relinquishing mind, harmonising without any self-conscious knowledge thereof, is the ultimate consummation of the Way.'[34]

Chapter 3

The artistic expression of Zen

These people have the same spirit as the ancients;
An earthen wall marks their separation from the world.
In the house volumes of poetry are piled on the floor.
Abandoning worldliness, I often come to this tranquil place
– The spirit here is the spirit of Zen.[1]

One of the most beautiful and interesting expressions of Zen for Westerners is through 'The Ways'. Although for some athletes this chapter may not seem so relevant, I feel that by examining these expressions of artistic discipline we can glimpse a little more of the spirit of Zen and consequently learn how to perfect our every action.

'The Way' (*Tao* – Chinese; *Do* – Japanese pronunciation) is a term which encompasses the traditional arts such as the Tea Ceremony, Flower Arranging, Poetry, Painting, Calligraphy and the Martial Arts, all of which are very highly regarded in Japan. Although in the West we might view these as being quaint and outmoded, this disciplined culture is the foundation of Japanese success in the modern world. Very often, individuals who have become accomplished in one of the Ways succeed equally well in other disciplines as they have perfected their mental state and can perform all activities with the same single-minded concentration. Examples of such people are Miyamoto Musashi (the famous swordsman and painter) and Ryokan (the esteemed poet and calligrapher). Equally important informal expressions of Zen are everyday routines such as polishing or cleaning; indeed all forms of daily work come into this category – whether or not they may be inspired or stimulating in their outward appearance. This philosophy permeates throughout one's life, each act performed as well as possible with disciplined simplicity and concentration.

No *work, no food*

The importance of normal everyday activities is illustrated by the story of a Chinese Zen master who used to work with his monks in the gardens even when already advanced in years. The monks, feeling worried that he was working too hard, hid his tools. The master stopped eating in accordance with his own teaching of 'no work, no food' until the pupils replaced the tools, after which he resumed working and eating as before. This is all so different from the Western approach where menial jobs are scorned and certain tasks are rushed and skimped in order to do something more worthwhile. These ideas may be illustrated by reference to the Tea Ceremony which is outlined in some detail later in this chapter; it may seem to many as a rather meaningless exercise, with its prolonged preparation and elaborate rituals, but the expression of discipline, attention to detail, calm mind and clear heart are what turn this mundane task into one of the most tranquil, spiritual and beautiful experiences.

In all the Ways, serenity and simplicity are mingled with the sheer joy of life and nature; the themes of brevity and impermanence are nevertheless always evident.

Calligraphy – Shodo

When one goes to Obaku temple in Kyoto he sees carved over the gate the words 'The First Principle'. The letters are unusually large, and those who appreciate calligraphy always admire them as a masterpiece. They were drawn by Kosen two hundred years ago.

When the master drew them he did so on paper, from which workmen made the larger carving in wood. As Kosen sketched the letters a bold pupil was with him who had made several gallons of ink for the calligraphy and who never failed to criticize his master's work.

'That is not good,' he told Kosen after the first effort.

'How is that one?'

'Poor. Worse than before,' pronounced the pupil.

Kosen patiently wrote one sheet after another until eighty-four First Principles had accumulated, still without the approval of the pupil.

Then, when the young man stepped outside for a few moments, Kosen thought: 'Now is my chance to escape his keen eye', and he wrote hurriedly, with a mind free from distraction: 'The First Principle.'

'A masterpiece,' pronounced the pupil.[2]

In the Ways, when Shin[3] is impure, when the need to impress or the desire for gain becomes prominent then the action becomes less than perfect. The mind is then disturbed, distracted, energy is dissipated and as a result we do not produce our best work.

Respectfully aware

There is a certain attitude to living life fully that is transferred into every action – respectfully aware, yet not formally so, slavishly polite; concentrated and alert yet not consciously contrived. It is important to live this way in everyday life, for trying to transform instantaneously a careless and undisciplined approach to life into creative artistic expression or athletic prowess is not possible. 'The attitude displayed during Zazen and the practice of calligraphy must be maintained in all the daily activities of walking, standing, sitting and lying. At all times, one must maintain full-spirited concentration.'[4]

Many calligraphers do not meditate or prepare themselves in any formalised way. For them, the actions of preparing the ink and smoothening the paper can lead to composure of mind and inner stillness. When finally all is prepared and everything is in harmony, then the paper is 'attacked' with spirit. There is no room for mistakes in Japanese calligraphy or ink painting. There is only one chance to produce perfection as the nature of the porous paper or silk is such that no retouching is possible:

> The preparation for writing (and later painting) is itself a ritual of almost religious significance. The ink, called sumi, must be prepared fresh each time it is used: a small amount of water is introduced into the concave portion of the ink-stone, and the slightly moistened inkblock is slowly rubbed against the stone, until the proper shade is realised. The brush is soaked thoroughly in water, dried by stroking it on a scrap of paper, dipped into the new ink and applied directly to the writing surface.[5]

The search for harmony

Other calligraphers, such as Chihiro Okayasu, do prepare themselves with more formal methods of meditation. This particular
artist sees her work as a constant search for harmony and the
perfect form. Through meditation and identification with the
object, she reaches a point where she no longer consciously
executes the work but rather her 'arm becomes an extension of
the brush'.

  Those rare occasions of harmony when the arm and the pen
are one, where 'it writes' (the pen takes over in an unconscious
flow), stand out in my memory of my Iranian experience with
Persian calligraphy. Here, the block of ink (*morakab*) was shaved
into tiny pieces and put into a tiny pottery container filled with
silken threads. A few drops of water were then added to this
and the bamboo pen (*ghalem-neh*) dipped into the container. Just
as the student in Japan copies the work of the master, so I too
would copy out line after line, page after page in an apparently
uncreative process. Then there would occur wonderful times
when I was lost in perfection, in timeless unity with the action
of the pen. I remember jolting back to conscious thought when
the teacher, smiling gently, moved his hands in a gesture of
finality and broke into French – in the manner of many elderly
educated Persians – informing me that it was finished, it was
perfect. Puzzled, I would ask myself why was it perfection on
this occasion and why not on the previous ten lines ... or on the
previous ten pages. I examined with my untrained eye the
curves of the Arabic script and thought maybe I could detect
some slight signs of better balance and smoothness of curves,
but no more than that. What really marked those occasions,
however, was my state of mind at those times when I seemed
to be in the 'zone'. Sadly I never felt that I mastered the art of
Persian calligraphy; that feeling of harmonious perfection occurred rarely, as in sport, as in most things – a fleeting period,
an oasis in a vast expanse of time. More often I was struggling,
straining, clumsily at odds with the graceful bamboo pen.

Persian garden

Hopefully, however, as in the study of the Ways, the journey
was the important process, not the goal. Those peaceful hours

spent in the house of the master or on my own, practising in my room at the embassy overlooking the walled Persian garden were of immense personal value. Any fear or anxiety about the violence of those troubled times in the early 1980s and the background bursts of gunfire or bombs, eased somewhat as I lost myself in the task of trying to recreate the beauty of the graceful Arabic script.

I tried over and over again to find a rational reason as to why I sometimes switched in to this all-encompassing 'zone' and sometimes did not. I was puzzled when one day I experienced this state very strongly after I arrived at the house of Ustad Abdolrasouli, feeling particularly tense. I had just undertaken a stressful drive down Pahlavi (the long avenue, now called Vali-e-Asr, traversing all the northern part of Tehran city) through the heavy traffic of revolutionary Tehran. This tense feeling is the antithesis of the 'zone', yet I know that some athletes can arrive at a competition on occasions in a rushed unrelaxed state and do particularly well. Maybe at these times there is no possibility of thoughts, negative or positive, no hesitation, a mind 'blanked out' by tension. I feel, however, that this definitely has a 'once-off' value and as a general rule, I certainly wouldn't recommend that approach.

Creative perfection

As a teacher, Ustad Abdolrasouli embodied so much of the Zen ideal, child-like but disciplined, his work and life an art of creative perfection. Although his long life had been anything but easy, he radiated happiness and people were drawn to him, attracted by his warmth and joy in everything. He was a Sufi scholar and his faith in Islam was a very important part of his life. His work, therefore, consisted mainly in writing Persian versions of the Koran and the poems of famous Sufi poets. His knowledge, talent and vast experience shone through his quiet humility and sincerity, and sense of fun. He would probably not have fitted the Western view of a successful man, totally lacking as he was in pomposity and glib certainty. Maybe this point can be illustrated by the following story:

A university professor came one day to Nan-in, a Japanese Zen master, to inquire about Zen. Nan-in served him a cup

of tea but continued to pour the tea even when the cup had
begun to overflow, until the professor called out, 'It is
overfull. No more will go in!'

'Like this cup,' Nan-in said, 'you are full of your own
opinions and speculations. How can I show you Zen unless
you first empty your cup?'[7]

This does not mean that we should take the easy way out and
avoid education and learning – indeed the calligraphy master
was an extremely erudite man – rather that we should always
be open to different opinions, never overtaken by our own pride
and self-importance, never feeling we alone have mastered
everything of value.

Ink painting – Sumie

The artistic expression of Zen could well be described as art for
art's sake. A sense of simplicity, space, spontaneous movement,
shading of light and dark, is the hallmark of Zen painting,
capturing the Oriental spirit which can make some of the more
stylised oil paintings of the Italian and Flemish masters look
heavy and dull.

One with the brush

In order to achieve this, the artist becomes one with the brush,
becoming the very object itself – no distinction exists between
the self and the pine trees, the mountain peaks and birds, rocks
and stones. The artist is in harmony with nature, no boundary
between the artist and the delicate beauty of the landscape.
When this happens, the painting comes alive for the observer
and the spirit of the landscape takes over so that, in the words
of the Chinese painter Chin Nung:

You paint the branch well,
And you hear the sound of the wind.[8]

If the body and mind are not in perfect harmony, not at one with
themselves and the task in hand, mistakes occur. This is illustrated by the story of Miyamoto Musashi, one of the greatest
artists and duellists in Japanese history:

Musashi was invited to brush a picture at the court of a
noble. He began the picture in front of everyone, but found

that he was overcome with nervousness, he that had faced a group of armed attackers without any fear. He tore up the picture and said that he would bring it the next day. He went home much disturbed and then faced the paper as if it were an armed enemy, throwing himself into the state of mind in which he went into his duels. The picture was a masterpiece.[9]

Only when the artist forgets that he or she is holding the brush – as finally 'it' paints – can perfection occur.

Imitation of the master

As in calligraphy, the Tea Ceremony and all of the Ways, the Zen way in painting is for the student to observe and copy the movements of the master, not to engage in discussion and argument. This can be particularly irritating to individualistic Westerners who feel it is a way of destroying their personal creativity. We should perhaps regard this silent repetition of the master's artistry as a training in composure and self-discipline, which will eventually lead to truly creative and spontaneous work.

  Margot Bohl, a student at Sophia University, who also started to study Japanese ink painting (*sumie*) and calligraphy while she was in Tokyo, describes the frustration of constant imitation of the *sensei*, which finally she accepted and learnt to continue 'in endless sessions trying to match him, observe his every mood and move, trying to feel like him, to feel the spirit of the picture, to grasp the message in so few strokes. And gradually, ever so gradually, some of his inner peace spilled over to me and I began to relax. I enjoyed just being near him.'[10]

  Many years later, when studying sumie in New York with Nanae Momiyama,[11] I recalled these words. Observing my tense hands and back, Nanae Sensei suggested that I should 'let go' and paint from the shoulder not the wrist. I attempted to follow her instructions in a mechanical fashion but found that I could only respond with stilted movements. Finally she placed her hand on the end of my brush and I felt the vitality flow from her touch into my arm. At this stage, deeply relaxed, the brush's movement started to sweep from my shoulder.

Total identification

Margot describes how she found it necessary when painting a leaf to learn to identify with the leaf, to feel its texture, experience the scent, observe the shades, notice its freshness and then 'as the artist participates in the drama of creation, she becomes the leaf, feels like the rain falling, and sails through wide open space with the bird she paints'. Margot went on to become a very proficient artist in Japanese ink painting. This concept of total identification is illustrated by Daisetz Suzuki in the following anecdote:

> The abbot of a certain Zen monastery wished to have the ceiling of the Dharma Hall decorated with a dragon. A noted painter was asked to do the work. He accepted, but complained that he had never seen a real dragon, if such really existed. The abbot said, 'Don't mind your not having seen the creature. You become one, you *will* be transformed into a living dragon, and paint it. Don't try to follow the conventional pattern.'
>
> The artist asked, 'How can I become a dragon?' Replied the abbot: 'You retire to your private room and concentrate your mind on it. The time will come when you feel that you must paint one. That is the moment when you have become the dragon, and the dragon urges you to give it a form'.[12]

This advice was followed by the artist and as a result a highly valued painting was produced on the ceiling.

Absolute nothingness

So when free from thoughts and distractions (*mushin*), the painter puts brush to paper as if nothing else exists, in a state of total harmony and absorption. This is what has been described by another author as 'a pure and composed harkening to that inaudible utterance, which yet subsumes in itself all things and which points to the absolute Nothingness lying beyond all form and colour (Chinese – *wu*; Japanese – *mu*)'.[13] Ironically, as we see time and time again both in artistic endeavours and in sport, from this state of Nothingness is born perfection.

The Tea Way - Chado

The Tea Way's essence
To boil water
to whisk tea and
to drink it – no more!
This is well worth knowing.[14]

Such is the spirit of the Tea Ceremony, just ordinary life, but at
the same time a deeply spiritual experience. It was at its height
with the Tea Master Rikyu, under the patronage of the military
leaders Toyotomi Hideyoshi and Oda Nobunaga in the six-
teenth century.

A fresh experience

In *Chado*, the reverent washing and drying of the tea utensils,
repectfully carrying them into the carefully prepared tea-room,
the gentle turning of the precious tea bowl on your hand, the
taste of the slightly bitter powdered tea – all add to the pervad-
ing sense of peace and harmony. In the tea ceremony, the simple
flower arrangement takes pride of place and antique pottery
vases from Iga are most highly regarded, although not ostenta-
tious in any way. Yasunari Kawabata, described the beauty of a
particularly highly valued flower vase in the following manner:
'The rough, austere and strong surfaces of old *Iga* take on a
voluptuous glow when dampened. It breathes to the rhythm of
the dew on the flowers.'[15]

The movements of the ceremony are performed with meticu-
lous discipline, each action done as freshly as if never before and
when finally the technique (*wasa*) is mastered, then and only
then can living spontaneity show itself. To many Westerners the
beauty of the Tea Ceremony may escape them and they see it as
a fuss about nothing. That however is, in some ways, the whole
point. In Zen, everything is important. The Tea Ceremony is
purely about making, drinking and sharing tea – a relatively
mundane action; yet each act is carried out as if it were the only
thing of importance to be done. Each act embodies a combination of constant awareness and respectful concentration which
is carried with one through life, not left behind in the inner
sanctum of the tea room. This is the spirit which shines through
the Japanese master and which was also recognisable in the old

Persian calligrapher. Only when free from needs and attach-
ment can an individual be really creative and able to produce
his finest achievements.

Week after week

Iwasa Sensei kindly gave me her small painted flat silk bag,
containing a tiny purple lacquered fan, with exquisite pink,
green and gold shading on the white paper, two small purple
silk squares, a tiny wad of rice paper and a small wooden stick
with which to eat the sweet cakes served with the tea. We
learned week after week, as a guest, how to hold the treasured
tea bowl correctly and to turn it gently as it rested on our hand,
sipping and then wiping with our silken squares, before passing
on to the next guest. When we had reached some proficiency in
this role, we then went on to learn to play the role of host: to
rinse and wipe the bowl to which we added the powdered tea
with the bamboo scoop, then adding the boiling water with the
graceful bamboo dipper. At this stage we whisked the mixture,
'gradually transforming the dry powder and boiling water into
a jade blend as exquisitely beautiful as it is harshly bitter'.[16] Then
bowing down, we offered the tea first to the main guest and then
to the other guests. Finally, we removed and stored away the
tea utensils with as great care as if this procedure were the main
ceremony itself. This again is an integral part of all the Ways:
the preparation and clearing away of the utensils are carried out
with great attention to detail, mindful of each action as if it were
the high point of the ceremony.

 After each session of formal training with Iwasa Sensei, we all
talked generally about European and Japanese culture, although we rarely discussed too specifically the Tea Ceremony.
The instruction was carried out once again by imitation. Not,
however, the stale copying we know in the West. Here it was an
open, living, breathing, sensing of the spirit of the master whom
we so respected. Just as the student painter or calligrapher
copies repetitively the actions of the master, so in the same
manner I learnt to observe and try to be at one with the spirit of
the Tea Ceremony. Often I felt awkward, stiffly and hesitantly
carrying out the formal movements which Iwasa Sensei performed so beautifully and with such dignity.

The Way of flowers – Kado

When I look carefully –
Nazuna is blooming
Beneath the hedge.

Basho[17]

The tiny wild flowers are unassuming, barely visible to the busy passerby but Basho's reverent appraisal of them make this *haiku* poem one of the most famous Japanese poems, for it 'proclaims the deepest secret of Nature, which is an artist's art' (D T Zuzuki).

The perfection of the self

I did not study *ikebana* formally in Tokyo. It was with interest therefore that I read *Zen in the Art of Flower Arrangement* by the wife of Eugen Herrigel. This book, by its very nature, could not have the same universal impact as her husband's description of his study of archery but it is, nevertheless, an interesting account of her own years in Japan in the 1920s and her intimate study of the skillful art of *ikebana*. In it she describes the same path as that trodden by all serious scholars in studying the Ways and explains simply but effectively the ineffable experience of Japanese art.[18] In this we discover the careful, conscious, disciplined preparation and repetitive training – and it is only in its wake that creativity can flow and take over. She recounts how her Western friends were amazed that she should spend so long learning this seemingly simple task and how she in turn was equally surprised at the superficial outlook which fails to see that the main aim is spiritual development – the perfection of the self and paradoxically, in the self's perfection, its very loss. As Daisetz Suzuki says in the introduction to the book: 'Yet mastery of the technique alone does not satisfy, we feel in the depths of our consciousness that there is something more to be reached and to be discovered.'

By itself, the formal technique, however perfect is wooden and lifeless without that spark of intuitive creativity which occurs when the self is negated and 'it' takes over.

Descriptions are made of the arranging of the implements used in ikebana, the bamboo stand and vase, pruning shears, saw and cloth and how everything was opened and carefully arranged 'in a timeless silence, every move of the hand was executed precisely and soundlessly'.[19] She started to imitate the wordless experience of the master, attempting to learn from his years of experience, gently bending branches, no forcing, no disharmony.

Composure of mind

She continued, as had her husband in his study of archery, patiently lesson by lesson, year by year, accepting the rejection of her efforts by the *sensei*. During all this period she attempted to make sense of the unfamiliar Eastern discipline, watching and sensing 'the unencumbered ease of movement with which a new structure took place under his hands in an unbroken rhythm of nature, life and art'.[20]

A lesson in the Ways, as she discovered, is not just a period of time positioned haphazardly in the midst of a chaotic day. It is necessary to prepare for the lesson by developing the correct state of mental composure. It is necessary to prepare oneself carefully giving all one's attention to the expression of inner balance and harmony, training oneself so that eventually this composure of mind becomes second nature.

Common thread

Activities as diverse as *kendo*, flower-arranging and painting are linked together by a common thread. Hours of careful preparation and unceasing repetitive training can lead to the pinnacle of successful performance through the state of 'no mind'. By attempting to obtain some knowledge of the Ways through self-transcendence and practice of the correct techniques, we may begin to gain some insight into the essence of Zen.

Chapter 4

The art of perfection in daily life

We must create our lives, free ourselves, become detached, simply attentive to here and now: everything lies in that.[1]

Creative state

The state of mind attainable during Zen meditation which I have been discussing in the preceding chapters can be described philosophically in several ways. That deep silence into which we descend is a form of pure existence – quietly breathing – the centre of everything, each breath the fragile link between life and death. This calm stillness is seen by Buddhists as Buddha-mind, by Christians as God. It can also be seen as the source of creativity or as the centre of healing. This is perhaps a semantic dichotomy – maybe these four concepts are the same, the fount of pure Being.

This profound stillness and silence, this state of pure existence, may be regarded as a state of healing. Consequently, at certain times, when in this state of relaxation, a feeling of healing power envelops the whole body. We can gain much by an analysis of Eastern healing methods.

The art of perfection

We have to learn to let go, to break down our barriers, to lose our attachments and let our creative spirit emerge. This we can learn from ancient Chinese wisdom. In one of his poems, Chuang Tzu describes the woodcarver's preparation which leads to the perfection of his art. He relates that the woodcarver, Khing, was making a bell out of precious wood. So perfect was this work that all wanted to know his 'secret'. He replied:

> I am only the workman: I have no secret. There is only this: when I began to think about the work you commanded I guarded my spirit, did not expend it on trifles, that were

not to the point. I fasted in order to set my heart at rest. After three days fasting, I had forgotten gain and success. After five days, I had forgotten praise or criticism. After seven days, I had forgotten my body with all its limbs.

At this stage the only thought that remained was that of the bell stand:

> Then I went to the forest to see the trees in
> their own natural state.
> When the right tree appeared before my eyes,
> the bell stand also
> appeared in it, clearly, beyond doubt. All I
> had to do was to put forth
> my hand and begin.[2]

For Khing there was no 'secret technique', no 'special method', just a disciplined training programme to achieve a state of pure thoughtless absorption – *samadhi*.[3] Obviously few Western individuals would – nor should they be advised to – emulate such a strict regime; nevertheless his poem embodies the spirit of perfect readiness for any performance or general pursuit. This state of mind, free from distractions relating to success or failure, fame or gain, certainly would be of advantage to many of us.

  Ironically, if we are not in this frame of mind, it is easy to lose our sense of the correct path to be followed. We are therefore often unable to see and seize opportunities, both material and spiritual, which are there for us to grasp. The woodcarver, on the other hand, was able to take advantage of the opportunity presented to him when confronted by the perfect tree. How many times have we been given opportunities which we have not taken or maybe not even recognised because our cluttered mind has hindered or clouded our perception.

Loss of creative energy

One of the fears of artistic individuals is that their creative energy may dry up and they may not be able to repeat the standards attained in their previous work. Obviously people go through different stages in their lives when they may be more or less productive. A lessening of creative outpouring need not, however, be regarded as the cessation of creativity, rather it may be a quiescent period when various threads are being re-organised and brought together at an unconscious level. It can be viewed not as a time to be feared but as a time to be accepted as a necessary stage in one's development.

Sometimes this creative diminution occurs at a time in our lives when we are undergoing major changes. We may need to accept this for a time and not resist it; when we feel ready, we can reset our goals and move on. If the process goes on for some time, however, or if there is a deadline for a piece of work to be completed, it would always be useful to have a mechanism which might lead to a speeding up of our creative recovery and which would help us move into the 'zone' more readily. First, however, we must identify our motivation, just as in sport we must train and develop our skills for the correct reasons. Imitative behaviour, spurred on by thought of gain or glory, will hold back our creative process. When in this distractionless state of mind, where the individual is totally enveloped by the work he is undertaking, then and only then can true creativity emerge.

Creative state of mind

I have outlined the following discussions with individuals who describe how they feel when they are 'flowing', in perfect harmony with their work.

Fashion design

This 'flow' state or 'zone' is of course universal and its application can arise in every career and aspect of living. One top Irish clothes designer discussed how her best collections were designed when she was in this state and in a fraction of the time taken to perform her less perfect work. Ironically, on these occasions her less-knowledgeable customers, seeing how little time was in fact spent on their commissions, sometimes questioned the quality of her designs. By contrast, when her work was seen to take longer and require a more laborious effort, it was often valued more highly by her clients although she herself recognised that it was by no means her best work. Like many of us, the designer could not easily identify the reason why she entered the 'flow' state on certain occasions. She felt, however, that it did not occur when she was under great time pressure.

She described how on one occasion, several weeks previously, she had been away on business and that evening in the hotel, 'I got a feeling that I just couldn't go wrong'. She drew out her spring range in a couple of hours and didn't have to redraw it. 'Normally it takes five to six weeks as I keep having to re-do it. This state of total perfection is very rare indeed.'

Musicians

Many musicians I have seen over the years have described their anxiety, which sometimes almost amounts to terror, when they appear in an important concert. At those times they forget their love of music and become obsessed with themselves and the impression they are making on others. As a result of this, they tense, strain and play less well than usual. At this time it is necessary for them to lose themselves in the beauty of the music, to have no boundary between themselves and their musical instrument and as a result to forget the audience.

This point is illustrated by a Taoist story:

> A wizard made a wonderful harp which was kept by the Emperor of China. No one was able to play the harp or produce more than harsh tones. One harpist, Peiwoh, started to play, he sang about the beauty of nature and the seasons of the year, he sang of love and he sang of war. When asked the reason for his success he replied, 'Others have failed because they sang but of themselves. I left the harp to choose its theme, and knew not truly whether the harp had been Peiwoh or Peiwoh were the harp'.[4]

The magic touch of the beautiful

This perfect sense of harmony was acknowledged by one New York woman as she described the Irish dancing competitions held in New York State. Tessa could easily tell by their perform-ance which children were in the 'flow' state and described how 'everything clicked, you could sense perfection in their whole being'. Her eight-year-old daughter Kate could recall this state on several occasions, remembering vividly that there was a great difference between these and other times because 'it felt so good and I didn't want it to stop, I could have gone on and on'. This concept was broadened by Tessa when she discussed how she herself attained the 'flow' state by watching them and it was almost as if she found herself transcended as she fused with this sense of perfection. Kakuzo Okakura refers to this idea when talking of the music of Peiwoh: 'At the magic touch of the beautiful the secret chords of our being are awakened, we vibrate and thrill in response to its call. Mind speaks to mind. We listen to the unspoken, we gaze upon the unseen.'

So too in our lives whenever we come into contact with any work of beauty or any perfect performance, by letting go of our ideas and emptying our cluttered mind, we can transcend ourselves and feel more alive and more complete. We can compare this sense of renewal and harmony with many other experiences which assail our senses in this modern age of mass media and sensationalism when, far from feeling enlightened we feel uneasy and diminished, our soul parched rather than refreshed.

Acting

Francine Roussel, who was one of a small group who created the Théâtre des Cinquante in Paris, has been working in New York for some years. We met one day in Manhattan for lunch in the East village, just before one of her new plays was being produced. Our aim was to discuss this whole concept of 'perfect performance' and to see in what way being a Buddhist contributed to her views. She was a delight to talk to, vibrant yet calm, her face serene yet liable to be transformed by a smile of pure joy at any moment. Francine had meditated for many years and meditation was an important part of her life.

Greed and arrogance fall away

She had found that when in the 'flow' state her performance would subtly change according to the mood of the audience. The composition of the audience, she found, changed depending on all sorts of things, such as the weather or political contexts. Some audiences would be much more sensitive than others to certain emotions. In the show she would sense this and if in the 'zone' she would act accordingly. On these occasions she described how everything would be 'magical' and the rest of the actors and actresses would be drawn into this perfection. 'When you have these great moments egocentric needs, greed and arrogance fall away, suddenly you are one with the universe.' At these times she felt that her performance and exchange of energy with the audience would have a greater impact than just affecting one small theatre. She thought maybe many of these 'perfect moments' experienced throughout the world – those moments of balance and inner peace – would lead one day to world peace. Hopefully she is right and this interest in spirituality as we head for the twenty-first century will mean that by each of us searching for perfection in our own lives, by each of us attempting to use our talents and abilities to help others not diminish them, we will reach out and the world will become a better, more stable place.

Every night at the theatre Francine found that there would be moments when some form of the 'flow' state took place and she described how 'you even surprise yourself, you feel so inspired'. Francine, however, was unable to be certain that she would achieve that state of mind on any particular night and, like so many people, she was unable to say why it happened on a certain occasion and not on others, although she felt it occurred at times when she forgot herself, 'a magical state occurred because we lost our self-consciousness and forgot ourselves'.

Public speaking

One college lecturer in New York, Nell Lauber, described quite beautifully how she experienced a 'feeling of lightness and a sense of being more fully alive' when she lectured while in the 'zone'. On days when she was not in this frame of mind she would be watching and judging herself, her ideas expressed less smoothly, articulating them in a more awkward way. In the 'zone' however, 'my thoughts came to mind more succinctly and clearly, interactions and connections seemed to flow smoothly and freely, there was a special sense of joy and exhilaration in simply being part of the very moment'. When we reflect on past lectures in college we can remember so many which were hesitant, awkwardly expressed and delivered in monotones by lecturers sounding more dead than alive. How wonderful, then, to hear this description so fresh, so full of vitality and clarity. The involvement of the lecturer was solely in the present, no worries about success or failure, just total joy in the task of communicating with the students.

The Irish television personality and university professor, Brian Farrell, discussed his mental state in relation to his lecturing and public speaking as well as his screen appearances. He described how, when in the 'zone', he is so clearly aware of the people in the audience that he could describe their reactions in detail but in no way do they affect him or distract him from his train of thought.

Mary Harney, the leader of the Progressive Democrats, a political party in the Irish Parliament, described how often she naturally achieves a state of 'flow' during her speeches. Like all people who try to achieve 'perfection of action', she prepares very carefully beforehand. She is determined to 'do a good job'. Mary feels that to communicate well with people she has to speak with integrity and is intent on 'being myself, not being pretentious'. Even with this approach and preparation, however, she doesn't always attain the state.

The most difficult occasions for Mary were answering questions live on television. She found that the times people felt she was at her best were when she was in the 'zone'. Like Brian Farrell at these times, 'I was aware of the audience but didn't react to them, nor was I aware of time passing'. On a bad day when she wasn't in the 'flow state', she discussed how she was aware of time dragging and of the reaction of the audience.

Obviously people like Brian Farrell and Mary Harney, in jobs which entail performance in 'the public eye', achieve this 'flow' state on a frequent basis; otherwise they wouldn't remain at the top for very long. Most individuals, however, still cannot guarantee that they will aways naturally achieve this state. In successful public speaking, as in any form of improvisation or acting, it is necessary to be in a state of *mushin* – to be without thought or distraction, free from the need to gain anything or to impress people, just passing over a 'message'. Many individuals need help in this area.

Writing
Well-known ornithologist John Terres, who has written many books on this subject, explains how he tries consistently to do

his best work. 'I have to become so saturated in my work and only then can I write with feeling – write from the heart – so that the book almost writes itself.' At the age of ninety John was always a delight to be with and his eyes would light up as he pointed out a blood-red cardinal and brightly coloured blue jay sitting on the lower branches of the tall pine trees in the lovely suburb of New York. Like all writers, he acknowledged that he could not achieve a perfectly concentrated state of mind every day. The most difficult time for him was when he started to write. He said, however, that he had learnt from Hemingway: 'I always stop writing when I am writing well and then I can pick up at the same place and sense that feeling again more easily.' Love of one's subject once again seems to be the main prerequisite for success. A desire to listen to the heart, not to imitate, not to do anything for gain but just for love.

Ray Bradbury in his interesting book *Zen in the Art of Writing* gives all actual and would-be writers some important advice: 'Work, relax and don't think.' He suggests that to get in touch with the real creative self it is necessary initially to rid oneself of thoughts of wealth and fame as well as literary acclaim, and soon 'The work after a while takes on a rhythm. The mechanical begins to fall away. The body begins to take over. The guard goes down.'[5]

How closely the advice of a twentieth-century writer echoes the words of the ancient Taoists and Zen masters!

Surgery

> The surgeon does not tell his scalpel what to do. Nor does the athlete advise his body. Suddenly, a natural rhythm is achieved. The body thinks for itself.[6]

Everyone who is doing a good job in whatever field must be aware of this state although obviously there are different levels of intensity. Dr Kami Fatehi, who was a leading Iranian neuro-surgeon, had, during the Iran/Iraq war, been performing as many serious operations in one week as his Western counter-parts would in a whole year. On one occasion in 1983, he was assigned for two months to Abadan, the oil centre at the top of the Persian Gulf, which at the time was the principal site of military activity, involving enormous carnage on both sides.

The city, with its huge oil refinery, was largely destroyed and he was there the night the Iranians broke through the Iraqi lines to relieve the lengthy siege. One cannot start to imagine the casualties involved at a time like that, not to mention the primitive conditions with inadequate supplies of food, clean water and medical equipment.

Fusion of mind – motor function

I learned a lot from my discussions with Dr Fatehi and obtained invaluable insights from him of the mental state required to undertake exceptionably intricate operations under unbelievably distracting conditions. Indeed, even without distractions, there is not much leeway for mistakes at any time in a discipline so precise as neurosurgery! When I met him again in the United States where he is now working, he described his mental state during his operations which normally take well over two hours to complete and can last as long as sixteen hours. He has suggested to me that, during this time, all bodily functions not necessary for undertaking the operation are stopped or reduced and his energy is directed into achieving his one and only goal in that situation – which is to bring about an 'acute, pure and perfect fusion of mind – motor function so as to obtain the best possible result for the patient'.

Over the years, Dr Fatehi has found that by his continued training and experience involving 'repetition and refinement' – like some of the top athletes – this perfect concentrated state becomes a natural occurrence so long as the goal of the best for the patient is kept in mind. Obviously, if financial gain or any other goal becomes a priority, then the actual quality of his work will suffer, just as in other creative work or sport. He describes how: 'In this "zone", the surgeon hears all normal sounds and sees all normal movements, and yet is not aware of them. With the least indication of abnormality, however, all signs surface in a conscious aware state so that some action can immediately be initiated.'

Constant concentration

Orthopaedic surgeon Dr John Shanley has led a fascinating life, including a spell as chairman of the Irish Red Cross. He informed me emphatically in 1995, the year of his 100th birthday that, 'when I was working I was always in that concentrated state of mind', and I am sure he was. He conceded, however, that this state was probably deepened whenever he was undertaking a more complicated surgical operation than usual. For fifty years he worked seventeen hours a day. This dedication and love of his work would ensure, I think, that constant perfect frame of mind. John Shanley worked in the Children's Hospital, Temple Street, Dublin, from 1923 to 1981 and was the Master there for many years. He also set up Cappagh Hospital in 1923 with Mr McCauley, in the house and grounds left to the Sisters of Charity by 'Humanity Dick' (a member of the Martin family of Galway). At that time, he explained, 'TB both pulmonary and surgical was a curse in Ireland and there was no cure'. Mother Cummins, who was in charge of Temple Street and a formidable woman by all accounts, asked: 'Why are we wasting this building?' TB patients at that time were being treated in Switzerland, so she brought down Mr McCauley from the North of Ireland asking, 'Why can't we do something too?' The First World War had just ended and she installed sixty military huts in the grounds and so began Cappagh Hospital.

Dr Shanley performed his last operation – the removal of a 'hidden' appendix – at the age of eighty-five. He was called in when the doctor performing the operation was unable to complete it.

Second nature

It is a very humbling experience to talk with people like Dr Fatehi and Dr Shanley, whose lives have been dedicated to the service of others. Maybe it is not surprising that the 'flow' state is second nature to them both.

These are the experiences of individuals describing how they function at their most successful times. As we all know, however, life is, unfortunately, not like that all the time. Even the people who appear to be most successful will acknowledge that a lot of extremely hard work over the years led to the apparently instantaneous success that we see. This is particularly so in sport; the winning of an Olympic medal may have been the culmination of ten or fifteen years' hard training. Sadly, for many people life is often more stressful than fulfilling. Many do not enjoy their work and are waiting for retirement when they hope to do all the things they've always wanted to do – but even these dreams are often never realised.

Part 2

THE ZONE IN SPORT

*When in the 'zone' I feel like a magnet
and the ball is like a piece of metal.*

Tony O'Dowd,
St Patrick's Athletic FC

Chapter 5

Zen in water sports

The way of water is infinitely wide and incalculably deep, it extends indefinitely and flows boundlessly far .... Beings cannot live without it, works cannot be accomplished without it. It embraces all life without personal preferences.[1]

Although many people may realise the relevance of a precise mental training programme for the martial arts, it may not be so immediately evident in apparently less precision sports, especially Olympic sports. Zen in relation to archery, for example, may seem much more relevant than attempting to relate Zen principles to swimming or sailing. Obviously the Zen programme must be changed and adapted for different sports as also for different individuals within sports. There is, nevertheless, a common thread running through all sports – and indeed all 'performances' and behaviour in other areas of life. Musicians, artists, writers, people involved in business life or indeed in any career, also need to approach their work in a relaxed, concentrated way in order to do their best and fulfil their potential. This chapter looks at several water sports and identifies times when focused awareness is crucial for performance.

~

SAILING

One day a man of the people said to Zen master Ikkyu:

'Master, will you please write for me some maxims of the highest wisdom?'

Ikkyu immediately took his brush and wrote the word 'Attention'.

'Is that all?' asked the man. 'Will you not add something more?'

Ikkyu then wrote twice running: 'Attention. Attention.'

'Well', remarked the man rather irritably, 'I really don't see much depth or subtlety in what you have just written.'

Then Ikkyu wrote the same word three times running: 'Attention. Attention. Attention.'

Half-angered, the man demanded: 'What does that word "Attention" mean anyway?'

And Ikkyu answered gently: 'Attention means attention.'[2]

Perhaps at first glance sailing would appear to be a sport which would not be too much concerned with concentration or 'zone'. Being technically competent and in control of a fast boat would seem to be the main components of the sport. Being fully aware at all times, however, is an important factor in all sports and in all ways of life, as Zen master Ikkyu portrayed so pointedly in the above anecdote. Indeed, Alan Beggs, psychologist to the British sailing team found in his research that concentration was the most important factor in sailing; the Irish team initially felt that the Zen programme would produce a form of 'tunnel vision', a type of concentration which would not be suitable to cope with the complex planning involved in sailing. A form of awareness where all extraneous factors are blocked out – apart from a narrow central field of perception – is not, however, the state of mind ideally achieved by a Zen-like approach; indeed, such a state of mind would not really be suitable for any sport. This is illustrated aptly by the Taoist saying: 'Those who comprehend the Tao are not focused only on themselves; they are also connected to the world.'[3]

The type of concentration attained in a Zen state of awareness is certainly intense, although all important aspects of the situation, such as weather conditions, race strategy, boat speed and tactics as well as other technical aspects, are noted and attended to as necessary. Olympic sailing coach, Trevor Millar, realising immediately the importance of being able to induce the 'zone' encouraged the team to adjust to the new concepts. They preferred to talk of refocusing and maybe this emphasis on the word focusing rather than the word concentrating is preferable because it implies total attention without the aspect of tension often associated with the word 'concentrate'.[4]

In the groove

Today, as in most sports, at the top of competitive sailing the
boat speed and technical knowledge of sailors are quite similar
and it is once again the mental attitude that makes the difference. The important points are, therefore, the ability to make
the correct tactical decisions under stress, not to be upset and
distracted by your own actions and the activities of the other
competitors and to do your best in your own race against
yourself. In sailing, that perfect state of mind where everything
flows and you know that whatever you do is going right is
called being 'in the groove'. One of the competitors describes
it as 'just slotting into a race, not attending to anything in
particular, yet at the same time being aware of the whole
picture', and contrasts this with other times (sadly more frequent) when 'you are actively concentrating on yourself and
your boat and worrying about the boats beside you'. Unfortunately for most people, in sailing, as in other sports, it is not
possible to slot into 'the groove' at will nor to predict when this
state of mind might occur. Many athletes say: 'Sometimes I get
that feeling and I don't know why, and as soon as I realise I'm
in that frame of mind, I have lost it.'

Marc Leveque, psychologist to the French Olympic sailing
team, suggests that there is more chance of obtaining this *état
de grâce*, as it is called in France, when you have made proper
methodical preparations. The first time this occurs, Marc
explains, the person feels fearful of the lack of control, this
fonctionnement automatisé. In fact I have found that athletes are
often afraid to talk to anyone about these experiences in case
people regard them as strange.

Decision-making process

Making tactical decisions is probably more crucial in sailing
than in many other sports. It is extremely important to be tuned
into the whole scene, aware of the wind and aware of what
tactics other boats are engaged in, but at the same time not to be
attending to or clinging on to these thoughts. It is necessary to
be sufficiently focused and alert enough to make correct decisions and yet be able to concentrate fully on the task of keeping
the boat up to speed. If, however, the wrong decision is made,

it is important not to get upset but to identify and rectify this as soon as possible. A point to watch for is the 'blinkered effect'. Having made a successful strategy in one race, it is important not to automatically follow the same one in the next race. The conditions may well be the same, but equally they may have changed, with possible disastrous results. It is important therefore, to make each decision carefully and take a fresh approach by utilising the available information about external conditions. One of the Irish sailors repeated the morning's successful strategy in the afternoon race only to realise too late that wind conditions had changed.

Consistency

The most important psychological concept in sailing is consistency. This is important in all sporting performance, but it is particularly important in this sport, as the final result in a regatta is taken from the overall results in several races. To attain good results throughout the week is obviously preferable to one top performance accompanied by a series of poor results. Consistency is obtained by a composed concentrated mental approach which does not allow the individuals to become elated by a good race or dejected by a poor one. It is interesting that when people start to use Zen meditation they often feel it is more important to compose and refocus their minds after a bad performance but do not initially realise that they may equally need the techniques after a good race. With more experience they understand that the elation following a top performance may be even more disruptive than the disappointment after a bad race and the excitement and accompanying physiological changes generated by success may be equally distracting by creating additional pressure for the next race. As Chuang Tzu remarked:

He who is wise ....
Does not rejoice in success
Or lament in failure
The game is never over
Birth and death are even
The terms are not final

Chuang Tzu[5]

Pre-conceptions

External conditions, such as the weather, can be of particular significance in sailing, especially as the sailors often have preconceived ideas about their abilities to sail well in both light and heavy weather conditions. This creates difficulties in that competitors then lack confidence in certain conditions, believing that they won't be able to produce the results. Once again the external events or conditions are irrelevant, it is the pre-conceptions which count. It may take only one bad performance in heavy or light wind to ensure that ideas are formed which may affect all future races. To regain confidence it is important to show that you can perform well in all weather conditions. Other events which may produce excessive anxiety or arrogance are, for example, the raising of the protest flag; this must eventually be regarded as just another minor distraction and treated accordingly. Some sailors also allow the boats ahead or boats alongside to be a source of apprehension and a negative influence which can act as a major distraction. It is important to be aware of tactics but to depersonalise the boat's occupants and continue challenging and testing against yourself – rather than others – as your own main rival.

Confidence

General lack of confidence comes from the concept that individuals sense that they have really not been doing their best. Therefore even a place in the Olympic games or several successes in competition may do little to encourage a genuine feeling of inner confidence. In such a case, good team spirit can prove very significant. A depressive or censuring atmosphere is not likely to lead to top performances whereas a positive supportive approach among team members and coach will encourage good results all round. At the end of the day each one must sail his or her own race; but performance is certainly enhanced if the competitor feels less isolated and more able to communicate hopes and fears – especially at the time of intense emotion preceding and after a competitive event.

Team spirit

A good team approach helps to cut out rivalry between members, which is of major importance, expecially in the situation where only one person can qualify for a certain competition. This can lead to an obsession with the rival's performance to the detriment of your own. The relationship between individuals in two and three man boats is also of paramount importance. Incidents followed by bouts of anger and resentment may mean the difference between winning and losing. It is very necessary, therefore, to pinpoint and sort out significant differences between crew members as early as possible, a task which – with a little communication and guidance – is often not that difficult.

SWIMMING

I began in what is nature to me, grew up in what is natural to me, matured by trusting destiny. I enter the vortex with the inflow and leave with the outflow, follow the Way of the Water instead of imposing a course of my own; this is how I tread it.

What do you mean by beginning in what is nature to you, growing up in what is natural to you, maturing by trusting destiny?

Having been born on land, I am safe on land – this is nature to me. Having grown up in water, I am safe in the water – this is natural to me. I do it without knowing how I do it – this is trusting destiny.[6]

Many of the central problems involved in sport have already been looked at in the section on sailing. The remaining part of this chapter identifies problems in several other water sports. When I first met one of the Irish swimming coaches, he could immediately see the relevance of such a Zen-type programme for power sports like swimming and pointed out many incidents in everyday life where energy properly directed led to super-human efforts.

Staying in the present

A major problem in swimming as in other sports is the inability to cope with distractions and remain focused in the present during training and during competition. Recurrent thoughts of past performances, especially failures and mishaps, tend to play a negative role and contribute to anxiety and loss of confidence in the hours and days prior to competition. In the water the swimmer may be worrying about the competitor in the next lane or the fact that her starting dive into the water was slightly out of rhythm. One top swimmer's concentration lapsed consistently if she broke the rhythm of her stroke by incorrectly executing her tumble turn, and she was then unable to put the event behind her and continued to think about this aspect of her performance during the race. She felt that, at times, she was more concerned with reliving her less than perfect turns than with completing the rest of the race. Her concentration had lapsed, her energy had been misdirected and as a consequence her speed dropped. Not only did she lose precious time by her mistake, she lost even more time worrying about it. A Zen approach teaches us not to focus on the past but to empty our minds of all distractions. As Miyamoto Musashi, one of the greatest Japanese swordsmen and artists, whose very survival on so many occasions had depended on perfect concentration, said: 'As far as I am concerned, I regret nothing.' In the martial arts of his era, a single thought – a fraction of a second – could mean the difference between life and death; what had passed must be forgotten immediately. That is not of course to neglect the necessity – once the race or competition is over – of analysing tactics and drawing the appropriate conclusions for future events.

Desperation to win

Another well-known phenomenon in sport is that of 'trying too hard'. The more desperately we try to do or get something, the more we strain to attain success the more it eludes us. As a Chinese sage remarked:

> There is a treasure in the deep mountains
> He who has no desire for it finds it.[7]

The more we let go of our need to win the better we can do. By trying too hard the swimmer strains and struggles, not flowing effortlessly but 'fighting' the water, setting up resistances against the water rather than being in harmony with it. When the swimmers are in the 'zone' they aren't aware of their bodies or the force of the water; some swimmers describe the experience as transcending their bodies and looking down on themselves. A top Northern Ireland swimmer, Marion Madine, described this experience to me and added: 'At this time there's only me and the pool, nothing else exists.' On other occasions, when not in this focused state, the swimmers are only too painfully aware of the sensations in their bodies and of everything around them.

Expectations

For some swimmers the expectations set up by being placed in a certain lane can be very disruptive. One young swimmer found that being seeded fastest in lane three, and therefore clearly expected to do well, was too much strain and she was often unable to perform at her usual level. Her concentration had been displaced onto expectation rather than performance. A similar state can arise when swimmers concentrate on the reputation or perceived ability of other competitors rather than on performing to the best of their own ability. In these circumstances, a swimmer is no longer swimming appropriately, but is concentrating on the performance of others to her own detriment. The usual pre-race anxiety symptoms affect many swimmers, even those who hold up quite well under pressure and can achieve a focused state of mind. They may find that during the warm-up they can lose the focused state when they permit negative thoughts to cross their minds or allow others to distract them even momentarily. It is useful to learn, therefore, how to maintain this focused state or to re-trigger it if lost. A lot of extra stimulation and crowd noise at many competitions can add extra pressure for individuals who prefer a calm, collected environment. It is preferable to learn to cope with these pressures in situ, since escape to the regained peaceful environment may not only be undesirable, it may well also be impossible. As Daikaku, one of the early Zen masters in Japan, says:

> The man resolute in the Way must from the beginning never lose sight of it, whether in a place of calm or in a place of strife, and he must not be clinging to quiet places and shunning those where there is disturbance.[8]

Starts are an important factor in successful swimming. Races are relatively short so that naturally every fraction of a second counts. It is therefore important to learn how to channel all your energy into focused, yet relaxed, dives and once again, if a mistake is made at this point, to put that thought aside. A slower start may sometimes be produced because competitors have preconceptions of their performance in certain events. For example, in the 400 metre race they may fear they will tire too quickly and, as a result, actually hold themselves back by worrying about this – thus getting off to a slower start.

Training methods

Northern Ireland swimming coach Bobby Madine, who is constantly devising new creative training methods, used a technique that has shown good results with his junior team. Before training he started to give his swimmers a 'pep-talk' on the concept of 'zone' – how in order to perform well they must be relaxed but mentally alert, each stroke must be flowing in harmony with the water, not separate and straining, each swimmer turning all the available energy into focused power and as a consequence swimming faster. Results showed that the team did in fact produce faster times when such talks were given beforehand. Dublin coach Carole Walsh devised similar methods with her junior team, and found that they helped them to 'let go' of needs and tense concentration and just swim more freely. As Lieh-Tzu points out in the quotation at the beginning of this section, the swimmer in the Lu-liang waterfall 'where fish and turtles and crocodiles could not swim' was able to swim himself by letting go, not forcing himself against the flow of water; he was able to 'do it without knowing how I do it – this is trusting destiny'.[9]

These ideas also helped the swimmers to maintain interest in training, a very important function as motivation can easily be lost at this time.

ROWING

No one uses flowing water for a mirror; still water is used for a mirror. By keeping thus inwardly, you become still and are not scattered outwardly.[10]

In rowing, which – if in single sculls – can be a solitary, lonely sport, the rower uses up great reserves of energy and there is a danger that he might burn out physically and mentally as he pursues his intensive training programme. It is rare in this sport for anyone to become world champion before his late twenties or early thirties, unlike Irish rower Niall O'Toole, who gained his title at the age of twenty-one.

Competing against oneself

Again, the role of self-esteem and the way the individual can cope with the other competitors is of paramount importance in rowing. Is the rower competing because he is desperately anxious to prove himself by beating others, or is he trying his best, competing against himself to realise his true potential in a sport he truly enjoys? Is he rowing his own race, or is he psyched out by the remarks of others before the competition, or do thoughts of other competitors, as they pass him by or even as he passes them, prove distracting? On one occasion at Ghent in 1991 when Niall O'Toole, the top Irish rower, was ahead of the world silver medallist for the first time ever in any event, he realised this fact half-way through the race, a thought which immediately distracted him. After the race, he explained the pattern of his thoughts at that time: 'I couldn't believe it, I actually was willing him to pass me because it seemed so incredible that I was ahead of him. I nearly made a mistake.'

In fact, by focusing on his breathing, Niall had begun to get such fast starts that despite this lapse in concentration he won easily. If, however, he had not been so far ahead of his rival it might have been a different matter.

External factors

The draw of lane, the difference in wind direction – these and other factors may all play a part in the general level of distracting factors. Many of them, however, are often not important in themselves, but prejudices and preconceived ideas about performance make them so. Very often, thoughts of one's past experiences under certain conditions interfere with one's current performance, e.g. 'I always do badly under these gusty

wind conditions, my opponent's lane is more sheltered', etc. As
a Chinese sage remarked:

> Just get rid of
> The mind that thinks
> 'This is good, that is bad',
> And without any special effort,
> Wherever we live is good to live in.[11]

It is important to see an event purely as an event, not coloured
by feelings of how we may react to it or how it might affect our
performance.

To get a fast start is definitely a technical and psychological
advantage. It is important, therefore, when on the starting line
to direct one's energy into one's performance, not into the
normal distractions. The rower who leaves everyone behind is
usually the one who is most focused.

Relax and settle

When a rival is catching up, the usual reaction is to try to
concentrate harder, to tense and struggle to maintain one's lead
by straining to speed up. However, once again the opposite is
achieved by these actions, and the sculler tires and slows down.
It is important to relax and settle, to let go of the need to strain
or to win, and to focus on one's performance. Admittedly this is
easier said than done – unless you have been training your mind
in this area. In Duisburg, Niall O'Toole found himself in the
unprotected lane. A gust of wind slowed him down, allowing
the competitor to catch him. He had to choose whether to concentrate on the wind conditions, his competitor, or his own
performance. He told me later that he was able to settle by
focusing on the stern of his boat and pulling away; meanwhile
his opponent, straining to catch him, 'burnt out' and fell behind.
This ability to relax and settle can actually lead to faster times, in
contrast to other occasions when the rower tries too hard, creating excessive tension in his muscles as a result of such intense
concentration.

In harmony with the water

As in other sports it is important to be in harmony with your
surroundings – one with the bow, one with the rifle. It is neces-

sary in rowing to be one with the boat, in rhythm with the water, not struggling against it. In boats with more than one rower, it is essential that they row as one, breathe as one and are in the same rhythm. The Netherlands Ambassador to Ireland, Eric Niehe, who competed with his national rowing team in the 1968 Mexico Olympics, described how he and the other members of the Dutch eight – as part of their pre-competition preparations – lay down, eyes closed, holding hands, and attempted to breathe as one man in order to get into a single rhythm. Another part of their preparation, designed to create greater harmony within the team (as well as an intuitive feeling of being 'one') involved the coach 'lifting the arm of the team member lying at the outside whilst the others had to sense that this was being done and then had to lift their arms at the same time'. All this was aimed at directing the focus on what 'your own crew is doing and not at what others are doing'.

The emotional relationship with team members within the boat is another factor. Obviously if the aim is to maintain harmony with the boat and to attempt to breathe as one, there should be relative harmony among the team members. The team members do not have to be good friends, but any element of disharmony can affect the common purpose, which is to row as well as possible.

CANOEING

Kasan was asked to officiate at the funeral of a provincial lord. He had never met lords and nobles before so he was nervous. When the ceremony started, Kasan sweated.

Afterwards, when he had returned, he gathered his pupils together. Kasan confessed that he was not yet qualified to be a teacher for he lacked the sameness of bearing in the world of fame that he possessed in the secluded temple. Then Kasan resigned and became the pupil of another master. Eight years later he returned to his former pupils, enlightened.[12]

Many competitors feel that they have perfected their performance because times or scores are excellent in practice or because they have beaten others in various competition. The true test, however, is when individuals can approach a top competition

– maybe one they have prepared for over many years, such as the Olympics – and not be thrown by the importance of the situation. Ideally each training period, each minor competition, should be approached with the goal of improving and fulfilling one's potential – although obviously in practice this may be difficult to maintain.

Flat water canoeing

In the sport of flat water canoeing, there are a lot of conditions which are similar to rowing and indeed all other sports. Intense concentration is necessary for a short period of time but, as one canoeist admitted, if this concentration becomes too tense – instead of relaxed but focused – then he actually slows down. As in rowing, by trying too hard to do well the competitor starts to strain and his performance suffers because energy has been divested from the main task of canoeing to the need to 'do well'. As Irmgard Schloegl points out in her story of a contempory Zen master, this can occur in all ways of life. When the master's pupils set out to please him he knew the opposite was about to happen: 'Their minds away on the great, they would forget the ordinary things such as opening or shutting the temple gates, and they burnt the rice, spoilt the vegetables and so on.'[13] Trying too hard does not have the right effect in any area. The competitor in desperation trying to be the best searches for new methods, new miracle cures without realising that the power for perfect performance is here in his own quietened mind, a mind that is free from distractions and intensity.

Emptying the mind

If possible it is advantageous to get a fast start, to empty one's mind of distracting factors and to harness energy to bring about the most powerful start possible. Rhythm is also important in canoeing, moving with the water, strokes looking and feeling effortless. Obviously individuals can also be psyched out both before and during the race by other competitors. If this happens, the canoeist is not concentrating on his own performance and is allowing himself to be distracted by individuals or past performances. On the water, one glimpse of a competitor coming into view can cause the individual to tighten up and to lose speed. Your attention should be focused on your lane, on your performance; you should be aware of other factors but not affected by them.

Slalom canoeing

This type of canoeing bears some resemblance to downhill skiing. Here the canoeist is racing against the clock but must also be careful not to make mistakes as he negotiates the gates at full speed.

In this sport there are two runs separated by a rest period, which is obviously a crucial time as regards one's reaction to performance. At this stage there is time for doubts to set in, so it is important not to allow oneself to get too elated by a good run or too depressed by a less then perfect initial performance:

> Take the world lightly and your spirit will not be burdened. Consider everything minor and your mind will not be confined. Regard death and life as equal and your heart will not be afraid.[14]

A single-minded approach

It is important to be single-minded and totally focused on the present. Success or failure should not be regarded as essential factors. Just as in the Tao of Lieh-Tzu, Confucius wondered at a man who practised with total dedication until he was able to catch cicadas with the greatest of ease:

> I hold my body like a wood-chopper hacking at a root, I hold my arm as steady as a branch on a withered tree; out of all the myriad things in the vastness of heaven and earth, I am conscious only of the wings of a *cicada*, I never turn about or fidget; I would not take the whole world in exchange for the wings of a *cicada*. How can I fail to catch it?[15]

Leaving nothing to chance by training sufficiently and becoming totally in tune with the canoe, conscious only of the stroke of the oars – how can one fail? As Confucius remarked on hearing the words of the man catching cicadas:

> Set your will on one aim,
> And be equal to the Gods.

It is also necessary here to have a good rhythm, to be in tune with one's self while negotiating the gates – smoothly and effectively but not hesitantly. Otherwise the perfect balance of maintaining speed without taking risks will be lost. Likewise, putting too much emphasis on the stop-watch in both training and competition can develop into a problem – here an obsession with seconds can hinder the canoeist from making proper progress.

Most of these problems are also present in other water sports such as wind-surfing and water-skiing, where there is the added problem of maintaining balance. Any lapse in focused attention in this instance quickly leads to the possibility of losing balance or even capsizing. It is important to be relaxed yet to maintain a totally focused mind in order to help the body sustain its rhythm and balance – once again to be in harmony with one's surroundings:

> In a contest, first control your own mind;
> Only after that think about technique.[16]

In this chapter, I have tried to show how a focused mind is as essential in all water sports as in other competitive activities. Trying too hard, being 'psyched out' by others or just one thought of self-congratulation or self-doubt may lead to inferior performance. Brian Greenaway was the coach for the Irish canoeing team in Barcelona and had been a highly successful coach to the British team for many years before that. He readily admitted to me that, in his experience, several Olympic and other medals had been lost in the past by teams he had been coaching, solely as a result of psychological factors. The first step is to identify where loss of concentration may be an important factor in each individual's performance and move on from there.

Chapter 6

Zen in general sports

BOXING

Chi Hsing Tzu was a trainer of fighting cocks
For King Hsuan.
He was training a fine bird.
The King kept asking if the bird were
Ready for combat.
'Not yet,' said the trainer.
'He is full of fire.
He is ready to pick a fight
With every other bird. He is vain and confident
Of his own strength.'
After ten days, he answered again:
'Not yet. He flares up
When he hears another bird crow.'
After ten more days:
'Not yet. He still gets
That angry look
And ruffles his feathers.'
Again ten days:
The trainer said, 'Now he is nearly ready.
When another bird crows, his eye
Does not even flicker.
He stands immobile
Like a cock of wood.
He is a mature fighter.
Other birds
Will take one look at him
And run.'

Chuang Tzu[1]

Acute pressure

The sport of boxing certainly encompasses all the usual difficulties associated with other sports – such as a desperate need to

beat an opponent and the problem of being psyched out by other competitors. Beyond those, however, there are additional elements including the fear of injury and feelings of great physical discomfort even before a fight. Each individual experiences differing amounts of tension at various times leading up to and on the day of the fight. It is important to identify these situations first of all so that solutions may be worked out to cope with them. One particular period of acute pressure is when the boxer has just come out into the arena and is preparing to put on his gloves. The week leading up to a contest may also be markedly stressful for quite a lot of boxers. During this period they may feel restless, under pressure or just more irritable than usual, especially as they are keeping very strict control over their dietary intake in order to maintain their correct weight for the weigh-in on the day of the contest. Inability to eat and drink adequately can also have an adverse effect on sleeping patterns, especially on the night before the fight, when they may only be allowed to rinse out the mouth with water to alleviate some of the discomfort. On the day of the fight the boxer may therefore be suffering from sleep deprivation as well as thirst and hunger. He may also have spent the night worrying about the fight, as a result of which he may well suffer a loss of confidence. Lack of sleep can thus be a major problem before a competition and one solution is to accept this situation and not fight it. The competitor can either relax using some form of relaxation exercises or do some other form of therapeutic activity. Leggett describes the old Japanese story of an experienced duellist who was sitting up with friends playing cards before a particularly difficult encounter. One of his friends said: 'Don't you think you should turn in? Your opponent is already in bed.' 'Yes,' was the reply, 'in bed but not asleep.'[2]

The important point is to keep one's mind free from negative distractions at this crucial time.

Possible injury
The boxer's confidence may also be affected by another factor, that of being drawn to fight against a more highly ranked opponent. The draw is a particularly stressful event for most

individuals; being selected to face the world champion in the first fight would indeed be a daunting experience for most competitors. In a sport like swimming or archery, the knowledge that world-ranking individuals are competing is sufficient to psych out some individuals, but it is much more difficult in boxing or judo, when the athlete has to physically engage the competitor. There is the essential problem of the very real fear of being physically hurt by the opponent. One of the boxing coaches suggested to me that this matter of possible injury should not be discussed with the boxers; he felt that the fear would be lessened by its denial. I feel that this fear, if not dealt with successfully, may seriously distract the boxer; as a result he may not be able to keep the crucial balance between offensive and defensive boxing, which may cause him to focus on avoiding punishment rather than meting it out.

Inner strength
Working on composure and confidence is of the greatest importance. The more calm and confident the competitor feels, the more will this inner strength be transmitted, not in a cocky arrogant way, but within a stable impassive demeanour. The overall aim is not to psych out others (I believe that those who actively engage in this are often dissipating their own energy in a negative way), but the competitor who is affected by neither success nor defeat will generally have a psychological advantage, as can be seen by some of the international teams who have brought this ability almost to a fine art – notably the Russians and Cubans, who over the years have shown little change of expression, whether winning or losing.

Overcoming fear
On this concept of inner strength, Deshimaru[3] tells the anecdote of the young Buddhist monk who was challenged by a Samurai to close combat. His master, telling him he would lose, instructed him in the best way to die. It was necessary to shut his eyes, raise his sword over his head and wait for death, which he knew would happen when he felt something cold on the top of his head. This the monk did. Observing this and not having experienced anything like it before, the Samurai himself became

very frightened, waiting to see what trick was in store. Finally, giving up, he begged the monk for instruction. The monk's 'secret' was not that he had special tricks but that he had no fear – accepting and waiting for death, he had emptied his mind of attachments to life. So also, the boxer who is confident and unafraid of losing, or who has no fear of physical hurt, has an advantage over his more fearful opponent. This may be true also for the underdog in all sports who, having no title or position to defend, may sometimes achieve amazing results. By overcoming fear, the boxer can actually become more controlled and decisive, less prone to defensively trying to avoid confrontation or flailing around, aiming punches indiscriminately. Similarly in life, being held back by fear or anxiety means that you do not live fully or achieve your full potential in anything.

Lifestyle and lack of discipline can be major contributing factors to problems in boxing. It is not easy in any sport to maintain, for long periods, the rigid training necessary to produce a top performer. But in a sport like boxing it is particularly difficult, where one's lifestyle is affected to such a degree that even the drinking of a cup of tea the night before a contest can have gigantic significance.

CYCLING

If someone asks what is the mark of enlightenment or
illusion,
I cannot say – wealth and honour are nothing but dust.
As the evening rain falls I sit in my hermitage
And stretch out both feet in answer.[4]

In the sport of cycling, it is important to have enough physical stamina to survive a gruelling seventy-kilometres race. Several factors may play a part here but excessive apprehension, in particular before a big race, may have disastrous effects on performance – from both the physical and psychological point of view. One young cyclist found he was so nervous that he was frequently physically sick before a long race – this physical disability of course added enormously to the other more obvious pressures involved. It is essential to examine the reasons that cause an individual to feel this way and to discover why this young cyclist turns what is normally for him an exciting experience into an extremely distressing situation. In this case the goal of winning or gaining glory had become all important; it had become necessary for his self-esteem to prove both to himself and others that he was the best. The process of cycling which he loved so much had receded into the background and become valueless.

Intuitive state of mind

It is not necessary to get a very fast start in cycling but, as in sailing, decision-making in the light of rapidly changing information is crucial, and pacing oneself can be particularly important. It is therefore essential to be in an intuitive state of mind in which all parts of the picture may be viewed, rather than simply to focus on one narrow aspect. Confidence plays a major role here; it often feels safer to stay with a group than to take a risk and break away. One cyclist lost a major race because she was afraid to 'take on the other riders – which I could have done quite easily'.

  There is often a conflict at work: one's intuition suggests one tactic and a rational voice suggests another. Marie Eribo, the Irish ladies cycling champion, was approaching the brow of a hill in one race when she had to decide whether to stay with the group or break away. Her intuition suggested to her that she should make a break, but she was also aware that the coach had previously instructed her that she should stay with the group at that point. She followed his earlier instruction, ignoring her own intuitive feeling, and too late realised that she had taken the wrong decision. It is very difficult for most people to learn to trust their intuition or even to identify it in the first place. Fortunately, when in the successful 'flow' state of mind, the intuitive voices often override all other messages and it is as if you are being guided and have no need whatsoever to question what should be done. Intuitively, therefore, you would know when to break and sprint away, and when to stay with the pack, pacing yourself correctly. Marie describes how the 'zone' affects her: 'I feel in control of myself and of the entire race and I can anticipate the moves of all the other cyclists.'

Aching muscles

In a long race in any sport a major recurring problem is a lapse in concentration in the course of the race. The cyclist may become aware of aching muscles in the thighs and calves and suddenly this feeling of pain predominates. Under these circumstances, the necessity of keeping focused on one's performance can easily be diverted into the new focus of concentration created by the often excruciating aches and pains. One of the top Irish cyclists began to realise that a particular problem time for her was the middle of a race when she invariably lost concentration. Her motivation was very strong at the beginning and at the end of the race, but she was prone to lose the race in the middle. By the time she had realised that she had slowed down it was often too late and her final burst of speed rarely made up the necessary time.

Over a certain period, negative distractions – even panic – created by the sight of other competitors may play a very important part in the failure to fulfil one's potential. Needless to say, the race should be regarded as over only when the finishing line is crossed; but the sight of a rival pulling away can often, unnecessarily, signify the end of the struggle for many cyclists.

ATHLETICS

Stubborn bird
Woodpecker at dusk
At the same spot.

Issa[5]

Perseverance

Athletics can be divided into many different areas but – irrespective of the individual event involved – the crucial issue, from a psychological viewpoint, is maintaining concentration: focusing all of your energy on the task of performing to the best of your ability. This performance must be maintained throughout the competition, when only a fraction of a second may separate the winner from the rest of the field; one glance over the shoulder, one distracting thought and the race is lost. It is essential therefore to persevere, to keep going, regardless of surrounding events, until the finishing line is passed.

Training is an occasion when lack of motivation or boredom may come to the fore, as the athlete trains day after day, week after week, with often only a single, long-term goal in view. For many athletes the tedium of the training programme obscures the purpose and enjoyment of their actual running, and consequently they may not fulfil their potential. It is important therefore to keep short-term goals in sight and to maintain one's focus on the concept of challenge and self-improvement. One of the most important factors is the ability to maintain the sense of enjoyment of the sport.

Runner's high

In running, a natural 'flow' state, frequently referred to as 'runner's high', can easily be identified. Mike Spino[6] suggests adapting Zen-like approaches or techniques to maintain a mental state conducive to peak performance.

Sprinting

A hasty attack is an exceptionally bad thing. The thing is to press aggressively only after having properly prepared yourself mentally and having observed the situation thoroughly once the face-off has begun. It is essential not to get flustered.

Yagyu Munenori[7]

Mental preparation

This quote by the seventeenth-century swordsman, Yagyu Munenori, shows the importance of relaxed mental composure in combat; this advice can be applied to athletics as much as to martial arts or combat sports. In sprinting, as in all events requiring short intense bursts of energy, such as canoeing and rowing, it is particularly important to get a fast start off the blocks. This can only be achieved in a relaxed but totally focused state of mind. Should there be excessive tension or even excessive relaxation, the sprinter could either have a premature start or be left behind. If the sprinter is thinking of the start or waiting for the gun, he may tense up and react more slowly. He may also react to the sight of the other competitors beside him with the result that he soon finds himself trailing behind them. The athlete must be totally in a state of poised readiness, energy focused on the here and now, and this state must be maintained throughout the short time of the race. This state can be seen by studying the way that some of the world's top athletes prepare themselves on the starting line.

On a recent television documentary[8], I heard Linford Christie, the British Olympic gold medallist, discuss his focused perform-ance in the Barcelona 100 metres final. Anyone who saw him run that race, could not but have been impressed by his single-minded and focused appearance. He described the preparations for the start of that race as follows:

> All I could do was focus. There were people wobbling and the noise was going on, so I didn't listen to it, I was just focused in on what was going to happen. And nothing was going to stop me from what I came out here to do.

This calm intensity contrasts greatly with a different form of intensity displayed by many other athletes on the starting line – moving, posturing, tension on their faces. 'Those whose words are humble while they increase war preparations are going to advance. Those whose words are strong and who advance aggressively are going to retreat.'[9]

Zen breathing

The sprinters I have been seeing were encouraged to learn to react in this focused way by concentrating only on their breath-ing while on the starting blocks; this would ideally result in what one of the Irish sprinters, Niall Fitzpatrick, described to me as 'my own cocoon of concentration'. Using suitable Zen breathing methods, it was my intention that the runners would be able to 'trigger' at the desired moment, i.e. the start of a race, the focused state of mind which they would have learnt to achieve in practice over the previous months. Niall describes this con-centrated state of mind as 'a slow-motion state where you feel totally relaxed and free of tiredness'. He contrasts this with occasions when he is straining to listen for the gun and, as a result, may react more slowly than everyone else.

Rival

Another major area of distraction may come from seeing a rival, which sets off thoughts like: 'He is faster than I am and maybe more talented; therefore I'm going to lose'. Often, of course, this other competitor may be under even greater pressure – in particular if he is the favourite and is expected to win. Nevertheless, by fixing our mind on other individuals we immediately put ourselves at a disadvantage. Having put in adequate training and preparations, we can then enter the competition fully confident that we will do our best.

> When you give up, or when you no longer want something, when you do not try to do anything special, then you do something. When there is no gaining idea in what you do, then you do something.[10]

In all aspects of running, the concept of trying too hard to produce fast times can come into play. Ironically, the more we try to speed up, often the slower we go. One young Irish sprinter, whose times had improved greatly in training, found that by concentrating on his times, he was not able to improve any more. The more he tried to go faster, the slower were the times he produced. It was imperative for him to take the psychological emphasis off the stop-watch and to start concentrating again only on his performance. It is necessary to let go of the desperation of needing to improve and let the action take over. The important factor here is the concept of 'letting go'. This illustrates the interesting paradox that excessive effort can sometimes lead to diminished results.

Middle distance

An explosive start is clearly not required in middle distance races, but in these events it is of course particularly important to keep the speed and rhythm flowing until the end. During races of these longer distances, there is more chance of the runner being distracted during the race, resulting in power being drained away into thought rather than action. The thought and sight of other competitors may play a major role not only at the start but also in the course of the race.

As in other sports, the draw to decide the position of individual competitors at the start of a race can be perceived as a problem.

One of the top Irish middle-distance runners felt that being drawn in the outside lane could be a disadvantage in the 800 metres. She also found that one of her main distractions was the constant thought of getting into a good position and thus avoiding being 'boxed in' or caught on the inside with no way out. Another distraction for her was learning her time for the first lap. This led to two types of distraction: 'If it is slower than expected, it takes away my concentration; and on the other hand if it is very fast, for a split second I hope I haven't gone too fast too soon.' Either way, being aware of her time became for her a disadvantage.

Distractions of the clock

Other top competitors felt that the clock was also a distraction for them. For one particular athlete, the main cause for concern would occur whenever a gap opened up between the race leader and herself. She appeared to spend more time questioning herself in such circumstances rather than putting all her effort into running the race.

Marathon

> What I point out to you is only that you shouldn't allow yourselves to be confused by others. Act when you need to, without further hesitation or doubt.[11]

In the marathon, the concept of a fast start is not important, but rather the idea of pacing oneself. The athlete must get into a correct rhythm, neither too fast nor too slow, and adjust this for bursts of speed whenever necessary. In fact this is rather like a decision-making process which balances intuition with action, when the individual is aware of those around but is not affected by them. There is no time for hesitation, even in a marathon.

A particular problem in any long-distance race is that of coping with pain, boredom and the consequent inevitable lapses in concentration. When in the 'zone' everything is forgotten, just as Bashō, tired from his wanderings, forgets his exhaustion when he sees the beauty of the tiny flower.

When worn out
And seeking an inn:
Wisteria flowers!

Bashō[12]

Pinnacle of training

At times when a focused state has been achieved, pain is rarely experienced. John Treacy, who won the silver medal in the 1984 Olympic marathon in Los Angeles, described this time as the 'pinnacle of training'. For him it is the description of a perfect race, a time when you are 'zoned-in totally', a time when 'no pain is involved, you are flying'. When the mind is perfectly concentrated on the task in hand, everything else fades into the background. The runner isn't even aware of his body; everything is fine, as acknowledged by an old Chinese saying: 'If the shoe fits, the foot is forgotten.' Again, John Treacy described to me his experience in Los Angeles when 'it didn't feel like hard work but afterwards I could barely walk'. It is crucial, however, to distinguish between types of pain – severe, unusual pain should be medically checked out.

Psyched out

Other competitors can obviously be a distraction and one Irish marathon runner found that she was 'psyched out' by competitors before and during a race. This would slow her down quite dramatically because it resulted in energy being withdrawn from her own performance and being wasted in turning her attention to the actions of other competitors. In the perfect mental state the competitors may often not be seen. John Treacy neither saw the crowd nor heard anything in Los Angeles. Dr Norbert Sanders, who won the New York marathon in 1974, was in this perfect state and didn't realise that he had passed Bill Rogers, a well-known marathon runner, who was in the lead and had beaten him into second place the previous year. 'The temperature was eighty degrees and the humidity was ninety per cent. Rogers was two minutes ahead with one lap to go. A friend gave me water and slapped my face, and as I passed the museum I heard yells that I was in the lead, I was dancing and I could have gone on for another five miles.'

On another occasion Norbert Sanders was in the Yonkers marathon. He had left his hospital bed that morning after a suspected appendicitis. Despite this he was in the 'zone' for most of the marathon: 'My body was gliding, I was floating in a capsule.' For the final few miles he lost the feeling of 'flow' and realised other runners were gaining on him. He won by several steps. The following morning the headline in the newspaper read 'Doctor Flees Hospital – Wins Marathon'.

For both of these runners the crowd and other competitors were an unnecessary distraction and therefore, were blocked out when they were in the 'zone'. An opposite case of attending to the crowd was pointed out in a story about Juan Manuel Fangio, the famous racing driver of the forties and fifties. At Monte Carlo in 1950 he avoided a multi-car shunt because, as he approached the blind corner around which it had occurred, he noticed that the crowd was not watching him, but looking in the opposite direction'. On this occasion Fangio 'tuned' into the crowd because their reaction was unusual and this difference was relevant to him.

On other occasions, as with John Treacy and Norbert Sanders, the response of the crowd was irrelevant – it was solely a distraction. In the 'zone' what is relevant appears to be attended to; what is not important appears to be acknowledged and then let go.

Race walking

Many of the problems associated with marathon running are very similar to those in race walking. Tactics are important; the athlete has to decide at what point to make a move from the group. It is also necessary to achieve a steady, fast pace and to be able to maintain it. One of Ireland's race walkers described how in the 'zone' he found that 'ultimately the rhythm takes you over and it controls you'.

In all races, at every distance, the problem of delays may arise. During this period, the competitor may become upset and nervous, giving the advantage to any individual who can cope well with the disruption created by any delay. It is therefore, very important to develop techniques to deal effectively with any eventuality such as a delay.

PARALYMPIC TEAM (ATHLETICS)

> As long as mountains exist, so there will be those who will
> need to climb to their summits. As long as there are those
> who are prepared to strive against and attempt to defeat
> the unknown, whatever that may be or represent, so there
> will be personal mountains to climb.[13]

When working with the Irish Paralympic team for Barcelona
September 1992, I found the same problems as for the able-
bodied athletes. They don't see themselves as different from
other athletes; their goal is identical – that of realising their
potential. Maybe, however, we should accept that their achievements are more than ordinary, if only because society is not yet
sufficiently organised to make life as easy for them as for their
able-bodied counterparts. I experienced this aspect of their lives
when they came to visit my office and I realised the great
problems which could arise for them simply transferring themselves from their cars to my house. They coped with such
difficulties on all occasions with good humour.

Track events
In the Paralympics, situations are similar to the able-bodied
athletic preoccupations; starts may be crucial, pre-competition
stress is distracting and a rhythm, in this case of pushing the
track chair, must be maintained.

Focusing on fears
Patrice Dockery described to me how she used to feel so
stressed she would get physically ill before her competitions.
Colette O'Reilly was equally stressed at these times. Both
women realised that their energy was being drained away from
their performance. Colette was not aware of ever previously
attaining the 'flow' state. This state of mind was recognised by
Patrice and she realised that at various competitions when she
had been in the 'zone' her performance had been excellent and
she had been very satisfied, regardless of whether or not she had
won. In fact on one occasion when she had got a medal she had
been upset because she had not really been 'flowing' and knew
that she had performed better in training.

Prior to Barcelona one athlete, John Fulham, came up against a common problem, that of finding his training very monotonous; as a consequence his times were getting slower rather than faster. He realised that he was concentrating on the end product, the games, rather than on the task of training. He was also focusing on his fears and anxieties rather than on enjoying his sport. John had been in the 'zone' only in flashes. Another young athlete, Mark Barry, had achieved this relaxed state of awareness previously but was still distracted by pre-competition nerves.

TENNIS

For nearly twenty years, he ruled without showing joy and anger; when the victory came he showed no elation: he sought for the truth of Zen and found it.[14]

Maybe these words uttered by Zen master Bukko about Tokimune reflect the essence of a central problem in tennis. The player who succeeds is usually the one who keeps calm and acknowledges with equanimity all stages on the path to the goal. Whether they are playing well or playing badly, most of the tennis players I have encountered over the years have tended to react to their standard of play with excessive emotion, which leads frequently to a negative effect on their performance. This obviously reduces the consistency of overall play; the crucial factor at this stage is to concentrate on the here and now – not the last shot or the next shot, not the outcome of the last game or the next game, but right now: this very shot. So did Tokimune, whose reign had been overshadowed by the threat of a Mongol invasion, learn to control his impatience and fear, and when finally the invasion occurred he was able to defeat the Mongols without any show of emotion. 'If you have the idea of superiority and are proud of your ability, this is a disaster.'[15]

The tennis player who is not expected to win may, when she realises she is ahead, lose concentration and in consequence lose the lead and, in all probability, the entire match. Once again our self-focused thoughts have interrupted our performance and the 'zone' has disappeared. Hillary Hough, the captain of Elm Park Tennis Club, described how this happened to him when on one occasion he was playing against an opponent whom he considered to be better: 'As soon as I realised I was ahead, I began to lose.'

One of the Irish Junior Team players, Orla Gallagher, found that initially she was easily psyched out by opponents whom she believed to be superior. During the game, however, she often came to the realisation, usually too late, that her opponents were indeed quite beatable. As the following poem illustrates, we place our own value systems and limits on life:

> Mount Fuji – Good in fine weather,
> Good in the rain:
> The Original form
> Never changes.[16]

We must go out to play our own game as well as possible. If we do this, unrestricted by thoughts or judgements of our own or our opponent's ability, then we may well win. This obviously does not mean that we do not assess realistically our own failings and strong points as well as those of our opponents – it means that, having done so and changed what is necessary, we are not held back by our own doubts or worries.

PARALYMPIC TEAM (TABLE TENNIS)

One of the Paralympics table tennis team, Siobhan Callanan, found that she was extremely sensitive to the remarks of others prior to competitions. It was therefore particularly necessary for her to remain extremely focused prior to and throughout the competition. Siobhan was for the most part an excellent player and often played in the 'flow' state, which for her took the form of an 'out of body' experience when everything in her performance became automated and she knew she was going to win. Over the years she herself had tried to induce this 'flow' state but found that while sometimes her attempts worked, more often they were less than successful. Attempts to induce the 'flow' state are beset by the same problems as attempts to win. The athlete desperately strains and the game is forgotten, muscles tighten, brows furrow in intense concentration – this is the antithesis to the state of relaxed concentration which ought to be achieved.

The advantage of triggering the 'flow' state through meditation is that emphasis is not placed on the mental state at all, instead it is put only on the meditation. Everday practice of meditation should make the 'flow' state a more regular occurence which can be triggered easily. Emphasis also is placed on just breathing and calming down. If the 'flow' state is actively sought it will not be found.

Getting rid of things and clinging to emptiness
Is an illness of the same kind;
It is just like throwing oneself into a fire
To avoid being drowned.[17]

Sometimes an athlete gets too obsessed with Zen or the 'zone' and this can cause problems.

The Hungarian Ambassador to Ireland, Dr Istvan Pataki, described how, as a teenager on his national table tennis team, he played blindfolded in order to sense the correct feel of the bat and ball, listening to the changing sounds of the ball against the bat, focusing on the intuitive aspect of the game. It is important to focus all one's energy on the task at hand not on distracting thoughts. Only then will true excellence be achieved.

Chapter 7

Zen in team sports

Behind a temple stood a field in which pumpkins were growing. One day the pumpkins fell to quarrelling. The heads divided into two parties, made an unholy row and insulted one another fiercely. The good monk who had charge of the temple heard the vulgar brawling and ran out to see what could be the matter. He discovered the pumpkins raging at one another and upbraided them: 'Pumpkins, you must be insane to attack one another like this! Start practising Za Zen this minute!' The pious monk showed the pumpkins how to practise Za Zen: 'Cross your legs, sit there with a straight back!'

The pumpkins did as they were told and while they were practising Za Zen their anger subsided. Then, as peace reigned, the Master said: 'Everyone now put his hand on his head!' They did so, and every pumpkin felt something extraordinary happening up there above him. They all found that a living runner went from one to the other, joining them together, and making them one plant. Ashamed of their previous conduct, they declared: 'How very strange. We are all joined together and all of us live one life together. And yet we went quite mad and started fighting one another. How stupid we were! Our good monk is quite right!' And since then the whole colony of pumpkins has lived in peace and amity.

An Edo parable[1]

We are more than self

Team games have all the difficulties associated with individual sports, but also the extra problems of working as a group. It is easier for a psychologist to work with individuals than teams. Working with teams involves a constant awareness of individual and group dynamics; it requires frequent checking to ensure that instructions are being followed correctly and that motivations are 'unravelled' and suitably directed so that the team works as a well-functioning unit.

One major problem that often occurs is that not every member of the team may see the relevance of dealing with psychological factors – when this happens any procedure is immediately rendered less effective.

When I was working with the Irish ladies soccer team several years ago, despite encouragement from manager Fran Rooney, only four team members were willing to consult me. Even seeing a few members of a team can be helpful, but it is certainly not ideal. Since then I have seen many teams and the whole team is usually willing to attend, but even so the actual response to the idea of working with a psychologist varies considerably from individual to individual.

Team spirit

Team spirit is a difficult concept to define, but it is essential. Openness, communication, support and harmony are essential ingredients, and the best results are often gained by those who play together for the common goal. As John Syer remarked: 'Teams may achieve success even when their members have no liking for each other or even dislike each other. Fulfilling the task set for the team is more satisfying to the members than the business of getting along with each other or making friends.'[2]

In order to promote openness and unity within a team it is important to have discussion groups where, in a supportive atmosphere, problems can be aired and solutions worked out. Major problems rarely go away of their own accord; usually, if not attended to, they fester and the situation may well deteriorate further when they resurface at a later date. From a psychological point of view the players who are particularly difficult to work with are those who are defensive and not willing to look at themselves honestly and admit to problems.

I have sat in on several pre-match meetings where St Patrick's Athletic coaches and trainers, Noel O'Reilly, Paul Nugent and Cyril Walsh, have discussed strategy and tactics with manager Brian Kerr, emphasising the important points. These meetings were very open and constructive, with a reliance on intuitive feeling for team selection. Many centuries ago Sun Tzu discussed the importance of strategy in regard to 'the art of war' and as one commentator, Zhang Yu, remarked: 'Therefore it is said that victorious warriors win first and then go to war, while defeated warriors go to war first and then seek to win.'[3]

Total support

Gaelic footballer and journalist, Liam Hayes, in his book describing his time as captain of the Meath team, explains the nature of the team spirit required both on and off the field.[4] He goes into considerable detail about the total support and commitment generated by the game – although he admits that Gaelic football is a sport which is sometimes tinged with a degree of tribal violence!

Most top athletes and team players also regard not only their own team but also their opponents with great respect, knowing only too well the amount of work and dedication required to reach that level of performance.

As mentioned by baseball player, Sadaharu Oh in an earlier chapter, an opponent is 'someone whose strength, joined to yours, creates a certain result'.[5]

It was interesting to watch members of the Irish boxing team point out the top Cuban boxers and describe their past feats with awe. They were not however overawed and were well aware of the skill and training needed to achieve such results. They felt that they too could achieve such excellence at some point. This positive attitude, I felt, was a factor in the Irish boxing team's overall good results at Barcelona.

In team sports, just as in individual sports, one of the most vital skills is to be able to control one's mental state rather than be controlled by one's emotions. This can be particularly important in a game like basketball or cricket which are team games but which involve also a series of individual encounters. Roger Fuller, an English cricketer, described how complicated decisions are required in cricket, decisions which can effectively be made only in the 'zone': 'The batsman has a fraction of a second to decide on the direction, trajectory and pace of the ball and to identify any spin that the bowler has imparted. All this information has to be taken on board in order that a decision may be reached on the initial movement to be made and the correct stroke to be played.' It is essential therefore to be able to capture that relaxed but concentrated state of mind which allows the

sportsman to 'read the game'; it is still thought by many that this
state of mind cannot be brought on at will. It has been difficult
over the years to persuade people that by letting go of the
concept of 'zone' but concentrating on breathing or other stages
of meditation it can be quite easy to trigger this state of mind.
This is because, as top American sports psychologist Robert
Nideffer[6] points out, very few athletes can get into the 'zone' at
will.

Leinster final

Liam Hayes described to me how he performed his very best –
when in the 'zone' – playing in the Leinster final (Meath against
their intense rivals Dublin). This was a game watched by 60,000
fans that is still remembered all over Ireland. He recalls running
down the field with the ball: 'The defence parted like the Red
Sea, I heard several players say "get him" and I scored. The goal
was so very close.' He pointed to the distance across the table
separating us, less than two yards. He then recalled how he had
watched the match on television that night and saw that the
defence did part to let him through. There was however, one
point on which his memory had been mistaken: the distance
from the goal-posts when he scored was not a couple of yards
but in fact was more than twenty yards. His feeling at the time,
however, was that the goal-posts 'had been so close that it was
impossible to miss'.

  Like many sportsmen, Liam had been reluctant to mention that
'magical feeling' to people because he feared he would be seen
as rather strange. This seems to have been quite a normal way
of viewing the 'flow' state: Marc Leveque, the psychologist to
the French sailing team discussed this with me at a regatta in
the south of France and agreed that the first experience of this
state often frightens people because they feel a little out of
control. Like Zen itself, the state defies adequate verbal description – it is necessary to experience it in order to comprehend it
fully.

SOCCER

In the hands of destiny

A great Japanese warrior named Nobunaga decided to attack the enemy although he had only one tenth the number of men the opposition commanded. He knew that he would win, but his soldiers were in doubt. On the way he stopped at a Shinto shrine and told his men: 'After I visit the shrine I will toss a coin. If heads comes, we will win; if tails, we will lose. Destiny holds us in her hand.'

Nobunaga entered the shrine and offered a silent prayer. He came forth and tossed a coin. Heads appeared. His soldiers were so eager to fight that they won their battle easily.

'No one can change the hand of destiny,' his attendant told him after the battle.

'Indeed not,' said Nobunaga, showing a coin which had been doubled, with heads facing either way.[7]

Confidence

Maintaining confidence is one of the major problems for all concerned. Even when the coach and manager know that the team has the potential to win, there may be some doubt among the players that prevents them from playing at their top level. Some players find that superstitious practices may help them but they have the problem that the loss of material objects or the occurrence of unpredictable events can easily generate a crisis of confidence. General Nobunaga was able to pull off this type of 'trick' because he truly believed, despite the odds, that victory could be achieved. This sense of belief must, of course, be genuine or the insincerity will be readily revealed. Management must work out their own methods in this regard. Some coaches believe that positive thinking will work even if the team is not playing that well. This, however, only compounds the problem, adding to the players feelings of doubt. It is difficult for the coaches to provide adequate words of encouragement if they know that their team is for various reasons, not performing as well as the rival team. This problem can be helped by a different approach to the concept of success. An attempt to move away from the concept of winning being all-important to the concept of improvement, fulfilment of the team's potential and the idea of challenge can very definitely lead to better performance. This is a better attitude in the circumstances; any possible self-doubt of the team is not magnified by the unhelpful views of the management. All can therefore work calmly together toward a realistic goal of team improvement rather than being distracted by a need to win. As Zen master Linji suggested: 'If you do not spontaneously trust yourself sufficiently, you will be in a frenetic state, pursuing all sorts of objects and being changed by those objects, unable to be independent.'[8]

Lack of unity
Just as in war, Sun Tzu recommended, 'So you should take away the energy of their armies and take away the heart of their generals'[9], so anger and demoralising remarks can lead to a deterioration in performance. One of the St Patrick's Athletic players, felt that his greatest reason for distraction was when other team players showed anger and shouted negative comments after a mistake had been made. As he pointed out, the players are quite aware that they haven't played well and are already distracted by that fact. Another player, Pat Dolan, suggested that maybe team spirit was only on the surface as there were too many negative comments during a match and it was necessary to check how deep the feeling of unity really was.

This important information came spontaneously in our first team meeting, and the manager and coaches pointed out that this was the first time the players had voiced dissatisfaction in this area and now this problem could be worked on. In fact, despite these comments, I felt that St Patrick's Athletic had one the best team spirits I had encountered. They had gone through a lot of financial difficulties over the previous few years and had seemed to be on the verge of disintegration for some time, having lost many of their good players.

Loyalty
They had been pulled back from the brink time and time again by Brian Kerr and his management's approach and there was a sense of intense loyalty, both among the players and the

THE ZONE IN SPORT

supporters. The pre-match and half-time speeches were also very productive. Brian was constructively emphasising the good points they should focus on, yet making them very aware of the negative areas and of the danger of a complacent attitude. This showed in their results: despite their disadvantages over the years, they always maintained a 'respectable' place in the league. Brian Kerr and Noel O'Reilly, referring back to their experience while training the Irish international youth team, pointed out that team spirit and the ability to concentrate can greatly compensate for lack of 'genius' in the team.

The reason Brian felt a psychologist might help was that although the team had not been losing, neither had it been achieving its full potential or getting wins. He knew it was now necessary to break the cycle of too many draws. He also felt that he had instilled too much sense of defensive play in the team recently because the way the league was structured meant that it was important to play cautiously and not lose, rather than to win. The result was that they hadn't scored many goals during the season.

Maintaining focus

In all relatively long team games, maintaining focused attention from start to finish is crucial. There is obviously no point in coming alive halfway through the match or, conversely, starting off in a concentrated frame of mind and then losing focus after a while.

For a short period after a break in play due to a player being injured or a goal kick for example, or towards the end of the game, there is frequently a time when a lapse in concentration is more likely to occur and a scoring opportunity can be presented to the opposing team who may then move in to attack.

Several times during the season, questions arose as to why certain St Pat's players, who were substituted at various points during the match, played extremely well. On other occasions when these same players were on the field for the entire game, they frequently performed much less effectively. This is unfortunately a well-known phenomenon that many people will recognise. As Liam Hayes pointed out in relation to his own Meath team:

Perhaps it was just coincidental that Mattie was more often able to re-enact the genius he had displayed on the training field whenever he was hurriedly introduced as a substitute midway through matches. Or perhaps, being told to remove his tracksuit and warm up on the sideline didn't give his own doubts time to develop.[10]

Dressing room
Dr Tony O'Neill, Director of Sport in University College Dublin and UEFA committee member, discussed with me the concept of 'psyching-up' in the dressing room. He felt that the noisier the dressing room, the less effective the performance, although he had found that it was often difficult to convince the players of this. I agreed with him that a quiet, focused state of mental harmony, with the energy channelled only into one's performance is probably the best way to prepare in any sport. It was interesting therefore that after my first session with his university soccer team, one of the players suggested that the Zen techniques might be successfully utilised in the dressing room in order to keep team members in a calm frame of mind.

RUGBY

When a thousand people are of like mind, they gain the power of a thousand people; when ten thousand people are of different minds, then no-one is really useful. Only when commanders, soldiers, officials and citizens operate as one body can they do battle in response to an opponent.[11]

Over two thousand years ago, the book of Huainan Masters laid down certain ideals for living based on early Taoist thought. So, many years later, we can gain something from their wisdom in the sphere of business, politics or sport. As Chris Pym, the Leinster rugby player, put it: 'When we play as a team, we all do well.'

This sense of unity as an essential factor in top performance was stressed to me by Roger Hill, a former member of the Australian Barbarians rugby team. He described how when the team was playing in a harmonious fashion, he found himself often in a state of mind which can perhaps be identified as the 'zone'.

When Ian Cairnduff, director of Dublin's Old Wesley rugby club, asked me to work with the team after the Barcelona Games, one of the players mentioned that because only a superficial sense of team spirit existed, this was a major problem for the team. A similar inability to form a sufficiently cohesive unit is probably a big factor in much of Irish club rugby. A successful team, whatever the sport, tends to be united in its aims and to 'operate as one body'.

Resistance

Wesley had not performed to their full potential over the years and like all teams everywhere they were very anxious to start doing well again. Unfortunately being too eager to win often leads to an inability to perform to one's potential. As an old Zen teacher said, 'As soon as there is any comparison of gain and loss, then there will be no end of wavering and compromise.'[12] Wesley had just hired an excellent coach from New Zealand, Ian Snook. It took time to break down resistance from members of the team. This was despite the fact that the team were aware that they needed a stronger psychological attitude. At one point after several sessions, one of the players, Greg Duffy, summed up for the group by saying: 'What we're actually admitting is that the techniques work but most of us are not using them.'

Concentration was, as usual, the main problem and each member of the team had to identify at what point and for what reason his concentration lapsed. For many players, the fact that they had achieved less than the best results over the years added to their loss of self-confidence. 'In one game, we were short of three regular players and, fearing further injuries, doubt crept in.' Doubts obviously can occur for many reasons, disrupting confidence and concentration. This is less likely to happen if the individual is in the 'flow state', but keeping that state for the length of a rugby match is not easy. Most individuals, if they can achieve that state at all, experience it in patches rather that for long periods.

Focused confidence

Ian Snook describes his approach to successful rugby: 'There are many facets which make a successful rugby player – technique, technical appreciation and fitness are three major components; but to enable them to be utilised fully, a player requires the ability to perform mentally, otherwise nothing is guaranteed on a regular basis.'

Together Ian and I worked on getting the team to quieten down just prior to a match. Until then they had been making as much noise as possible in the dressing room in order to convince the opposing team and themselves that they were full of confidence. The stillness they hoped to achieve would, of course, not be the silence of nervousness but the calmness of a focused confident approach.

Another point brought up was that of playing hesitantly and defensively, reacting to other teams rather than initiating play. Chris Pym said: 'I've seen it for years ... we just wait and see how the opposition are going to play, then we react to it, if it's not too late.' Chris decided that 'our focus needs to be on imposing ourselves in the first quarter and to do that we need to be playing more aggressively and with more inner determination.'

Come-back

The team felt that losing motivation and concentration were hallmarks of their recent play which would 'tail off' easily at some point during the game. Although a 'come-back' might occur by this stage it could possibly be too late.

The coach felt that increased strength and power was required in the scrum and we concluded that this might best be achieved by a combination of breathing techniques along with some form of visualisation.

FIELD HOCKEY

Once your basic mind is settled, you should just tune and order it, making it calm and stable, undisturbed by events not deluded by prospects of gain. Watch for disorder and clamour among the enemy ranks, then attack.

Du Mu.[13]

Intense concentration

The problems involved in hockey are obviously similar to those in other team games. Several years ago one of the girls on the Irish ladies soccer team found that her meditation techniques could be used equally well to bring about an improvement in her hockey game. Hockey is an extremely fast and skilful game. Intense concentration is required for long periods of time and this concentration can easily be disrupted for many reasons.

Before I moved to New York, I worked for a short time with Glenanne hockey team. The team coach Eddie O'Malley was very aware of the 'zone', which he personally found easier to attain in indoor hockey games. One of the players, Gerry Shaw, found that he was 'thrown' by grass pitches, or by certain umpires with whom they had experienced problems in the past. On one occasion when in the 'zone' he remarked how it had been raining heavily all day, but 'I didn't notice rain in the game. I couldn't tell you if it was raining'. There was already a very good spirit in this team evidenced by their support for one another on and off the field. Nevertheless they felt that if they could synchronise their play more effectively, be more in harmony – then their game and results would improve. If they were playing in this truly harmonious, focused way, doubts would not materialise so frequently.

Drained

Some of the team described how at certain points in the game – often after the first five or ten minutes – they felt 'completely drained'. This was a time when they tended to lose concentration and made mistakes. Rory O'Donoghue found that he needed a psychological 'trigger' to maintain concentration at these psychological turning points. Another point at which many players were 'lulled into complacency' was after a goal had been scored. They would often at that point tend to 'sit back', thus increasing the possibility of a strike by the opposing team. Another player suggested that it would be necessary to identify these periods and work together as a team to overcome them.

The role of the goalkeeper is especially onerous as in many team games. Throughout the entire game he may have to touch the ball only a few times. Maintaining concentration through these idle periods can be a problem for some individuals.

Susan Mullaney, hockey player and coach, highlights the importance of players and coaches seeing the necessity of a strong sense of team spirit. She points out the importance of each player taking responsibility for the quality of her play, not only for her own sake but because of the effect it may have on the other members of the team.

In all sports the time leading up to the match is particularly prone to feelings of self doubt and anxiety. It is very necessary to adopt a mental training programme which will help players to deal with pre-match nerves.

BASKETBALL

> When people are skilfully employed, they are like the legs of a millipede – numerous without interfering with each other. They are like lips and teeth – hard and soft rubbing together without hurting each other.[14]

When any team is playing as one, in harmony with one another, they function together effortlessly, just like the legs of a millipede. There is no friction, just a common goal.

For a short time I was working with a New York college basketball team. The majority of the players recognised the relaxed aware state of mind, the 'zone', and were able to describe how they achieved their best performance in this state – 'I felt so confident on the court, I felt that I could score almost at will. Shots that I would normally not make were going straight through the basket; it was an incredible feeling.' Several students stressed that they had entered the 'zone' more frequently in high school. Most players achieved this state very rarely and agreed that this meant that their play was inconsistent. On some occasions they achieved flashes of brilliance, 'effortless, light, can't miss a shot'. At other times they played badly. As one player put it: 'The final whistle can sometimes last a lifetime; that's when you've lost.'

One high-school student, Kieran Darcy, pointed to many occasions when distractions could occur. Reacting to others – whether players on the same team, opposing players or the crowd – can be a major factor. He pointed out, however, that 'when in the "zone" I don't know the crowd exists'. Needless to say Kieran felt that a close-scoring or play-off game were also particular times of pressure.

  The problem discussed here and the description of peak performances are common to all team sports, although individuals will experience the 'zone' in their own unique ways.

Part 3

THE TECHNIQUES

*To regulate the mind, it is necessary
to regulate the body – the breathing and the posture.
In this way it is possible to store up physical energy
and unite it with mental energy.*

Tomio Hirai,
Zen Meditation Therapy
Japan Publications Inc (1975)

Chapter 8

Mental training programme

*Tense people spend too much of themselves. Their efforts are
excessive instead of economical and efficient.*

Edmund Jacobson

There are many relaxation methods which you can learn from
books or tapes which will enable you to choose the form which
best suits you.

When I originally put together a programme for sport, Jacobson's 'progressive muscular relaxation technique'[1] was used
because I had found this to be the most effective method of
relaxation when treating various types of anxiety states over the
years in my clinical work.

Jacobson was a pioneer in this area and started his investiga-
tion in 1908. He found that most people, in those days, associated recreation and hobbies with the word 'relax'. Even today,
so many years later, many people feel that they are automatically
relaxing when they watch the television. This of course is not
necessarily so. We may be sitting hunched up or cross-legged,
with our muscles displaying a great deal of neuro-muscular
tension. Tension means that our muscle fibres are contracted.
Relaxation, on the other hand, implies the perfectly natural
occurrence of lengthening the muscle fibres – contractions and
movement are absent and neuro-muscular electrical activity is
subdued. The method devised by Jacobson demonstrated that
relaxation is a natural process, and teaches individuals how to
recognise tense or contracted muscle fibres by tensing muscle
groups all over the body and then relaxing them. After practising this contraction and relaxation technique for some time,
muscular relaxation becomes automatic, like any other task of
muscular coordination.

When I first started treating anxiety patients at Queen's University in Belfast, I found that subjects were able to relax their muscles extremely well by using Jacobson's method; after some time, however, they tended to find it much more difficult to calm their minds and to curb their mental distractions when trying to imagine themselves in the midst of some peaceful nature scene. When I returned to Ireland from Japan I felt that one way to alleviate this problem might be to introduce a stage of Zen meditation from time to time throughout the relaxation process. This appeared to be successful for most people who find that the meditation helps to calm their minds quite effectively and appears to deepen the relaxation process.

The following instructions are from an adapted form of Jacobson's progressive muscular relaxation which I have been using. I have found it useful to divide this sequence into two sessions so that the first – arms, shoulders and neck – can be practised for several weeks before continuing with the rest of the body.

Find a room that is neither too hot nor too cold and wear loose clothing. Remove shoes and settle back in a comfortable easy chair, putting your feet on a stool. Breathing should be natural and unstrained throughout. Inhalation should occur when tensing the muscles, and exhalation while relaxing them.

SESSION A (Do each of the following sequences three times)

Right hand and arm: Clench your right hand, making a fist, then bend your elbow. Clench your hand and wrist, at the same time tensing the forearm and upper arm, while bringing the clenched hand up to the shoulder. As you do this you should feel an increased sensation of tightness in all of the muscles of the arm. Be aware of the tense sensation of your muscles for ten seconds. Slowly let your arm down, unclench your fist and straighten your elbow and relax your hand. Now be conscious of the relaxed feeling in your arm. Let the sensation of tension drain away, concentrate on the relief of experiencing this feeling of deep relaxation. Now do the same with the left hand and arm.

Both hands and arms: Clench both fists and bend and tighten fully both arms together this time. Feel the tension in the fingers and in the lower and upper arms. Now gently let the tension go.

Relaxed diaphragmatic breathing: Breathe from the diaphragm[2] in and out through your nose. Imagine a tiny feather on the end of your nose and as you exhale, breathe so gently and gradually that you do not dislodge the feather. The exhalation should be a little longer than the inhalation. Breathe deeply but not in a strained way for three or four breaths. Concentrate only on the feather.

Shoulders and neck: Put your hands on your shoulders and tense the muscles across the upper back by elevating the shoulders and making slow circular movements with the elbows, tensing as you lift and relaxing as you lower. Feel the tension in this area of your shoulders and upper arms. Gently let the tension go and experience the feeling of relaxation.

Lift your chin and stretch your neck as much as possible in so far as you feel comfortable and feel the tension at the back of the neck. Lower your head to a relaxed position and push your chin onto your chest, experiencing the tension under your chin. Raise your head again to a relaxed position.

Turn your head to the right, feel the tension at the right side of the neck. Relax in the central position, experience the relief, the relaxed feeling, and turn your head to the left. Experience the tension on the left side of the neck and gently relax in the centre.

Again inhale from the diaphragm, breathing through your nose for three or four breaths, concentrating on the imaginary feather on the end of your nose. Now imagine you are on your own, lying or sitting in some location which you find relaxing – by the sea, or by a stream or in the country. As you relax in your special place the sun is shining and gently warming your skin. If you feel your mind getting distracted, return to the breathing and concentrate on the image of the feather. Practise this sequence for one or two weeks if possible, once a day, especially when you need to feel refreshed. If you wish to practise at night it is a good way of helping you slide into a relaxed state of sleep.

SESSION B (Do each of the following sequences three times)

Feet and legs: Point your feet away from you, be aware of the sensation of tension in your calves. Now relax your feet, feel the relief as the tension drains away. Pull your toes towards you, again experiencing the tense muscles in your feet and calves. Relax the toes and feel the relaxation as your feet gently flop outwards.

Lift your right leg slightly off the stool and extend it away from you, pointing your toes and stretching as far as possible – experience the tension in your thigh muscles. Gently let the leg down and notice the feeling of relaxation. Repeat the exercise with your right leg.

Breathe deeply in and out through your nose. The exhalation will be a little longer than the inhalation. Breathe out so gently that you do not dislodge the imaginary feather on the end of your nose. Breathe three or four times and concentrate on the feather.

Buttocks and abdomen: Tense your buttocks and pull them in under you. Notice the tension in your hips and thighs – let the muscles go and experience the feeling of relaxed muscles.

Pull in your stomach muscles – feel the sensation of the tense muscles and then let them sag. Experience the relaxed feeling in the area of the abdomen. Now try to tighten the stomach and buttock muscles at the same time, then relax both muscle groups at the same time together.

Inhale through your nose from the diaphragm, then gently and gradually exhale without dislodging the imaginary feather at the end of your nose. Breathe three or four times.

Face: The facial muscles are among the most difficult to relax and are very important at times in that they can instantly betray your emotional level and state of tension. This can be vital in sports where a relaxed, composed psychological image may be crucial and a tense, ill-at-ease competitor puts himself at a psychological disadvantage right away.

Tense up the forehead area – be aware of this feeling of tension and then imagine a pair of hands gently smoothing away the wrinkles. Concentrate on the relaxed feeling.

Tense up your eye area by frowning – concentrate on this sensation and then relax. Be aware of the heavy eyelids closing lightly. The most relaxed position for your eyelids is drooping heavily yet gently – like stage curtains falling down, lightly closed, not tightly clamped shut.

Concentrate on your mouth. Purse out your lips – be aware of the tension around the mouth. Now let go and concentrate on the feeling of relaxation.

Clench your teeth, feel the increased tension in your jaw area, then unclench your teeth and feel the relaxed feeling in your jaw.

Open and widen your mouth to the side – be conscious of the tension again as you contract different muscles – and now let the tension go. Be aware of your tongue sitting comfortably in your mouth and your lips gently closed with a small gap between the centre. This is the most relaxed position for the mouth.

Breathe deeply in and out from the diaphragm – so gently and gradually that you do not dislodge the tiny feather perched on the end of your nose. Breathe three or four times.

Now imagine yourself sitting or lying on your own in a relaxing location, beside the sea or a quiet stream in the countryside. You are feeling totally relaxed and the sun is gently warming your skin. Again, return to the breathing and concentrate on the feather if you begin to think distracting thoughts.

After you have practised this sequence daily for several weeks you should be able easily to recognise your tension points and relax automatically. Jacobson also identified the concept of *differential relaxation*, by which we learn to be aware of different muscles, which we wish to tense, and others which we may wish to maintain in a state of relaxation when carrying out some activity. Start to identify the various muscles which need to be relaxed during various activities and practise this when sitting or moving around. This concept is particularly important in sport so that only necessary energy is expended and there is no additional energy loss from the tensing of muscles whose services are not required at that time.

It should now be possible to identify when you are deeply relaxing instead of convincing yourself that watching the television is automatically a relaxing process. This form of progressive muscular relaxation can be used at any time when you need to feel refreshed. If you have difficulty sleeping then this sequence should help you to sleep better and – even if you do not fall asleep – a period of relaxation during the night is certainly preferable to lying awake worrying about the following day.

SECTION 2 MEDITATION

A 'graduated' programme of Zen meditation offers a way to help to achieve successful performance in any area, and especially in sport, by assisting us in achieving a focused state of mind. I can describe this mental state as special because when we actually try to achieve it, it eludes us; if we have achieved it and think about it or try to hold on to it, it disappears. Nevertheless it is, in fact, a very natural state of mind – an ability to absorb oneself in tasks and activity and to perform well as a result of concentrating fully and not being distracted by fear of failure or the need for success. It is, in the words of the Zen monk, Ryokan, a 'mind so clear'.

 Many years ago, I came across various descriptions of successful mental states – 'be positive, keep calm, keep your mind on the task' – but few directions as to how to achieve these states. Now, many years later, there are several good mental training programmes. Unfortunately, techniques for improving concentration – probably the most important requirement – are still not in adequate supply. The most effective method for improving concentration and coping with distractions that I have found is a form of Zen meditation. By disciplined training in this area, the mind can learn a constructive approach to various forms of distracting stimuli, whether external (other competitors, weather conditions) or internal (anxiety symptoms, fear of vomiting).[3] The mind learns to acknowledge a distraction and to let it go. The emphasis here is on letting go, not on clinging to and elaborating on the thought, nor on straining to push it away. Breathing deeply and naturally in an unstrained way and learning to sit in stillness lead eventually to an ability to maintain a state of one-pointedness, a harmony between body and mind.

Distractionless state of mind

In this programme the individual is involved with three components of meditation training – in general life, in training or practice and finally in competition. Thus his ability to achieve this distractionless state of mind becomes a way of life, not some technique dragged out tentatively on the day of the competition. It is of course not easy for Westerners to achieve this goal, living as we do in a culture so at odds with the ideas of selfless discipline and so much more in tune with instant results and arrogant posturing. It is nevertheless worth the effort. By practising at home the individual starts to learn how to cope with all the trivial distractions which assail the mind. He can then start to use this as a preparation for training and finally, on the day of the competition, all the usual doubts and fears and physiological responses can be viewed in the same way as a trivial distraction and treated accordingly. The techniques can also be used as a trigger to reinstate at a time of stress or lack of concentration those feelings of focused relaxation which have become so familiar in training. This can give a feeling of control to the athlete, allowing him to take responsibility for his own body and mind, rather than being controlled by them. Control, in fact, is the important word for most of the athletes who have used this programme successfully.

Aimless aim

In archery, when the archer is eager for success or fearful of failure, he strains at the clicker, his back and arms contorted in tension and his arrows loosed in a conscious, jerky way. When his mind is composed, the breathing is correct and the arrow becomes one with the bow, slipping away like 'ripe fruit off a tree' or 'snow sliding off a branch'. There is no strained movement, no inappropriate tension, just 'everything flowing' – a calm, tranquil moment where nothing distracts the archer from his performance, his 'aimless aim'. The meditation energises the personality; it helps the individual to focus his mind, which is much more alert and aware of what is going on but able to lose itself in action, while his body is nicely relaxed, as the perfect dancer moves naturally in time with the music, no thought of what to do, no stilted movements, lost in the music and in the moment.

Similarly in sailing, Conrad Simpson, one of the top Irish sailors, used this technique frequently to help him look around and make the correct technical decisions, aware of but not affected by external events or emotions. We are thus capable of giving ourselves fully to whatever we have undertaken. This is perhaps one of the most important factors in successful living and is normally so difficult to achieve. By doing this, however, everything can become more enjoyable and be more successfully undertaken. Everyone knows how time appears to fly when we are concentrating and fully immersed in activity, and how it drags when we are flitting from thought to thought and action to action, only half alive. As we go through the meditation stages, learning to breathe correctly and concentrate fully on each breath, so we are not aware of our goals but remain goal-less – the future takes care of itself. All we have is each breath. This might be interpreted by the Westerner as drifting – it is, in fact, the very opposite; we are grasping the immediate moment, being aware of the here and now. For example:

> A lord asked Takuan, a Zen teacher, to suggest how he might pass the time. He felt his days very long attending his office and sitting stiffly to receive the homage of others.
>
> Takuan wrote eight Chinese characters and gave them to the man:
>
> 'Not twice this day
>
> Inch time foot gem.
>
> This day will not come again.
>
> Each minute is worth a priceless gem.'[4]

Our aim must be to do our best to fulfil our potential, not to waste precious talents or time, the most valuable commodities we possess.

Zen meditation programme

> You should know that those who like easy things are, as a matter of course, unworthy of the practice of the Way.
>
> Dogen[5]

This meditation programme I have adapted from a number of sources[6] and from my own experience over the years. The posture for the body during the exercises is not the usual lotus position but a simple Western sitting position. The more usual Eastern positions can be found in many books, but I feel that this can sometimes add a feeling of doing something different, something esoteric, which may interfere with the process itself. What we are setting out to achieve here is a relaxed concentrated state of mind – 'ordinary mind' – no more, no less. On the day of a competition we do not have to display outwardly to others what we are doing – our mental training programme; indeed, if we do, it might well put additional pressure on us to perform, not less. What is necessary, however, is the commitment and discipline to practise this programme daily. I have tried to make the programme as simple as possible but nothing worthwhile is too easy, as Dogen pointed out in the twelfth century.

Correct position

Choose a quiet room, at least when you are starting (later on you will be able to cope with an increasing level of distractions). Sit on a hard-backed chair or stool – not leaning against the back of the chair – feet squarely on the ground, hands flat, palm-down on thighs, just above the knees, back straight, head straight, with eyes looking down a metre or so ahead. Use a chair of the correct height, if possible. It is better not to sit on a patterned carpet, which may prove too distracting. Wear loose clothing and do not look at a watch. Do not stare at a spot or pattern; let your gaze be diffused; you are focusing internally, not externally. If you feel anything strange, just stop meditating – you are perhaps hyperventilating or straining your breathing, or staring fixedly at something. Any 'visions' or visual distortions (makyo) are definitely not to be encouraged! When you have finished, move your body around loosely and stand up slowly.

How to breathe

Inhale deeply from the diaphragm through the nose, exhale through the nostrils, allowing the exhalation to be a little longer than the inhalation. Breathe deeply but do not strain; do not raise your shoulders as you are breathing. If you have difficulty breathing through your nose for any reason, close your mouth in a relaxed postion – lips closed with a tiny gap in the centre – this should aid your nasal breathing.

How to deal with distractions

When you are faced with a distraction (as you frequently will be) learn to acknowledge it, to look at it and let it go. Do not push the thought away, do not cling on to it – quietly let it go and then gently bring your mind back to whatever stage you are concentrating before you were disturbed. Eventually thoughts will pass in and out of your mind, not attended to, just there.

Stages of Zen meditation

Guidelines for length of time of each stage: Obviously this is an individual programme and what is correct for one person will not necessarily be right for everyone. It is important to find which stages are right for you but it is equally important to give each stage a proper chance and not to move on purely through boredom or through lack of discipline. As a general guide, stage one may take three to four weeks, other stages six to eight weeks.

Stage one: counting. As you exhale, count one silently on the first breath, elongating the sound to fit the length of the breath if you wish, count two on the second exhalation, count three on the third exhalation, four on the fourth exhalation and five on the fifth exhalation. Return to the count of one and repeat to five. Do this for five or ten minutes, concentrating on the counting.

Stage two: rhythm. As you inhale, say to yourself, 'I shall breathe in'; as you exhale say, 'I shall breathe out.' This should produce a gentle rhythm on which you concentrate.

Stage three: waves. As you breathe in, imagine waves lapping or crashing against the shoreline, and being pulled out again as you breathe out. Concentrate on the rhythm of the waves.

Stage four: feather. Imagine you have a tiny down feather on the end of your nose and, as you exhale, do so as gently as possible, so that the feather is not dislodged. Concentrate only on the feather.

Stage five: music. Listen to a piece of music which you feel is right for you. Many people find flute music appropriate. Concentrate on the music. Lose yourself in it as you breathe gently.

Stage six: breathing. Follow the passage of the breath as it passes down to your diaphragm and back out again and concentrate on this.

Stage seven: moving Zen. *(Kinhin)* (This is done in a formal way with very slow structured movements of the feet in time with the rhythm of the breathing. It is used to ward off tiredness in between periods of *zazen*.)

  Walk with a good but relaxed posture, arms loosely at your side, and fit the rhythm of your breathing into the walking.

Stage eight: *hara*. Breathe in through the nose and when the lungs have been expanded, mentally push the breath down into the lower abdomen/*hara* (of course, the breath is actually escaping gradually and gently through the nostrils). Concentrate on the pushing-down movement.

Stage nine: *tanden*. Breathe in and push down as in the previous stage but concentrate on the *tanden* (area one inch below the navel).

Stage ten: polishing. Make polishing movements with your hand flat on the table in front of you. Use large circular sweeping movements. Concentrate on the *tanden*.

Stage eleven: Blank mind – allow your mind to go blank as distractions come and go unheeded.

Deep concentration

Greater power and stability have been experienced by those athletes who have progressed to the *hara* stage, although many had initial difficulties. The procedure accordingly is outlined here in some detail for those who may have problems in mastering this stage:

Breathe in deeply and gently from the diaphragm. Then push down as though pushing breath down into the *hara*, although in fact you are gently letting out the air through the nostrils – concentrate on the action of pushing down the breath. If you feel your breathing is too strained, loosen your shoulders and let your abdomen protrude somewhat (while still maintaining a good posture).

Most athletes have found stage two (rhythm) very helpful. Combined with stage eight (*hara*), it can produce a very deep form of concentration.

As I stressed earlier, this programme has to be adapted for each individual and the different stages would appeal to some people and not to others. Some archers, rifle-shooters, golfers and sailors have found the 'feather' stage particularly useful. One of the archery team concentrated on the imaginary feather on the end of his nose as he exhaled. He transposed this onto the sight pin and found it a very effective way of 'letting go' of the target and achieving a perfect release of the arrow, whereas previously his rigid obsession with the target had muscles to tense and he had been unable at times to loose the arrow.

The moving or walking Zen (*kinhin*), is useful for maintaining focus during preparation or non-competitive parts of a contest – such as the collection of arrows in archery or in the intervals between shots in golf.

I recommend, however, that – whatever combination of stages is finally decided upon – it is advisable to begin with the counting stage.

The calm, concentrated state of mind which should result from following this programme can be utilised as a basis for many achievements. In sports, this focused state can help the athlete to achieve peak performance.

SECTION 3   PSYCHOLOGICAL CONCEPTS

The Need to Win

When an archer is shooting for nothing
He has all his skill.
If he shoots for a brass buckle
He is already nervous.

If he shoots for a prize of gold
He goes blind
Or sees two targets –
He is out of his mind!

His skill has not changed. But the prize
Divides him. He cares.
He thinks more of winning
Than of shooting –
And the need to win
Drains him of power.

Chuang Tzu[7]

Success and failure

It seems obvious that the driving ambition for those involved in competitive events is to win. Indeed our culture has conditioned us in such a way that any competitor who suggested he wasn't interested in success would probably be regarded with amazement and suspicion. Since childhood we have always had the notion of success instilled into us, failure must be avoided at all costs. This, of course, does not take into account the different aspects of winning. The winner may not be pleased with his performance or may even have cheated or taken drugs to reach the top; success in those cases is not, in my opinion, worth attaining. In some cultures there is a sense of dignity in failure, a concept which in the West we find difficult to understand. In Japan, a noble hero is one whose 'single-minded sincerity will not allow him to make the manoeuvres and compromises that are so often needed for mundane success'.[8]

Elusive

An equally disturbing idea to the Western mind is the suggestion that one way to gain success is by not trying to win. This has finally been recognised, though not yet always fully accepted, in sport. It is relevant, furthermore, to many other areas of life. The more we desperately strive to gain or achieve some thing the more elusive becomes the desired objective. This can be seen whether we are taking exams, applying for jobs or forming successful interpersonal relationships. If we are relaxed and really not anxious about the outcome of a job interview, then we are much more likely to create a good impression and be successful, than if we feel desperately in need of this particular job. Obviously, this does not imply a total lack of interest in what we are trying to achieve. Rather it involves an interplay of tensions, achieving the right degree of motivation with relaxed detachment. A need to achieve may, by increasing arousal, so disrupt our mental and physical performances that ironically we do not succeed. This paradox takes a prominent position in the logotherapy of psychiatrist Viktor Frankl[9]. He suggests for example that the more one wishes to obtain happiness the less happy one becomes. In his terms, the state of happiness is seen as a by-product of leading a meaningful existence rather than a goal in itself.

Compete against oneself

More recently, his logotherapeutic approach has been applied to sports. Frankl himself states that the important thing in sports is not trying to defeat others but attempting to do one's best and actualise one's potential, ie compete against oneself, not others. One of his techniques, which is very effective both in psychotherapy and sports, is paradoxical intention. How it may be successfully used in sport can be illustrated by the following example, which occurred on the occasion of an important competition, the shoot-off for selection of the Irish archery team to the Moscow Olympics.

Phil had shot his arrows extremely well and suddenly realised that he, a relatively new competitor, was shooting at world-class level at a time when the standard in Ireland was not very high. This was an idea too exciting and frightening for him to accept calmly and he immediately went into a state of uncontrollable shaking. Throughout the day he attempted to control his shakes but the more he tried, the worse his shaking became and, of course, his score suffered accordingly. On the following day he was instructed to shake as much as possible, to try to increase, not to fight, the shaking attacks. When he attempted this his attacks stopped and despite his score disruption on the previous day he won the competition by a large margin.

On another occasion, Phil had been attempting to shoot in the laboratory in front of the coach and several members of the psychological team. When asked to try to obtain perfect scores for his next six arrows, Phil was unable to hit the gold once and his overall score was very poor. He was very dejected and wanted to give up, but was then told to shoot again just as before but this time to make sure that on no account was he to hit the gold (an easy achievement, looking at his previous performance). A change immediately came over him as he exchanged his dejected look for a confident appearance, stating that it was an impossible task; if he was shooting at the target, he must hit the gold. He then proceeded to do so five times out of six, his sixth arrow just barely missing the centre gold!

Self-orientated thoughts

What is the phenomenon that induces performance disruption in sport and indeed in other areas of our lives? A crucial factor is that of self-focusing. Self-orientated thoughts have been found to be a major distraction in sports. Here the attention is directed away from the task onto preoccupation with autonomic functioning and self-evaluation. This problem can also be seen in other sorts of task performances, and is a major factor in many aspects of emotional problems where it involves a preoccupation with a problem and an inability to concentrate on other facets of one's existence.

Selfless

Perhaps one solution might be a detachment of oneself, becoming selfless. The Japanese are more familiar with this concept than we are and on this foundation of selflessness are built many of their strongest traditions, such as the martial arts, the tea ceremony and the Samurai code of Bushido. In sport terms this concept may be most clearly seen in the distinction between performance in a contest and performance while practising. Some athletes are capable of displaying a very high performance on their own during training. However, when performing with team members or in competitive functions, they are unable to achieve their previous success rates. Once again, self-focusing mechanisms take control and interfere with the athlete's level

of concentration. We become preoccupied with personal problems or self-image and the task is no longer of primary importance. As Chuang Tzu noted so long ago, 'When we become
preoccupied with a need to win, then that desire drains us of
power.'

Perfection of action

Some of the main concepts relating to peak performance in sport
and indeed successful living may be identified as simple themes
developed over the decades by various humanistic psychiatrists
and psychologists such as Frankl, Maslow, Fromm and Jung
although, as we know, these themes were developed many
centuries before by sages in several countries. One way I like to
look at this experience is as William Johnson described it to me
– 'perfection of action'. Maybe we could see a Zen approach to
life as the art of perfection.

Starting with this concept of success and failure, I have found
over the years that one of the quickest ways to motivate individuals is to give them a pattern of those themes which they can
analyse and adapt for their own performance.

Doing your best

Over the years, the concepts touching on success and failure
have played a central role in my work with athletes and others.
I have always used the concept of doing one's best as an ultimate
goal in sport, rather than concentrating on winning or achieving
a definite time or score. For me, this means performing a task to
the best of one's ability and concentrating on the journey towards self-improvement rather than on the outcome. Many
individuals in sport are naturally very proud of their particular
sport and see any problems as unique to their sport. Basically,
however, the core problems are similar in all sports.

The difference between Japanese and Western thought,
here, is that the Japanese are more interested in gradual
improvement and are somewhat bemused by the Western
need to become an outright winner or an instant expert. Even
the word 'expert' is not used much by the Japanese because
of its implication that everything is already known and

achievedandthatfurtherself-developmentisnolongerthought
necessary.

You are your own rival

In practical terms, this concept means concentrating on fulfilling
your potential rather than on being involved with the performances of the other competitors. The person against whom you
are competing is yourself, not a rival from your own or another
team. Worries or thoughts of others act as distractions, interfer-
ing with the improvement of your own performance. That
dissipation of energy or lapse in concentration may well be vital
during the competition as it may mean a loss of a fraction of a
second in a speed sport or may allow a 'hit' which finalises the
contest in a combat sport. If this lapse occurs just before the start
of a competition it may also be responsible for undermining
your own confidence. Anything, therefore, which acts as a
distraction from enabling you to fulfil your own potential is
contributing to a less than successful performance, whether
such distractions take the form of thoughts of success or failure
or concern about other competitors.

Reaching spiritual development

The Japanese Zen culture, over the centuries has, of course, been
imbued with this idea of performing your utmost as an act of
perfection and spiritual development, rather than for any gain
or for the defeat of others. Ironically, though, this has enabled
them to become world masters in many areas, such as the arts,
sport and business. The more you intend, or attend to, beating
the other competitor the less likely are you to do well. The less
interested you are, therefore, in triumphing over others, and the
more focused and relaxed you are, then the more likely are you
to succeed. This can be applied to most sports.

   One of the sailors who was overly concerned with the prowess
of others started to depersonalise the other competitive boats
and occupants, regarding them as blocks of wood bobbing up
and down on the sea and consequently posing absolutely no
threat to him. This technique worked very well for this particular sailor, although it might be necessary for others to devise
their own personal symbolism. One of the swimmers, as he

stands on the starting blocks, runs his eyes up and down the swimming lanes in order to limit and define his lane and psychologically cut out the other competitors.

Chance to learn

Some coaches and psychologists are critical of this central goal of 'doing your best' rather than a goal of winning, beating others or achieving a specific score in competition; they feel such an approach is too vague and not sufficiently specific to be useful. This may be because of ambiguities of meaning in the phrase. For me it means trying to fulfil your potential by putting all your committed energy and concentration into your actions and performance at that time. This is totally different from some vague hope of performing well. Even if your best performance is not achieved, it is not a reason for becoming upset but rather a chance to learn. Each performance in training and competition should be regarded as a learning experience, not a cause for either elation or despair. You either succeed or you learn – you never fail.

Effortless beauty

Getting the correct balance between doing your best and trying too hard is of paramount importance. The concept of excessive effort implies elements of strain and desperation, neither of which is conducive to good performance. Excellence stems from relaxed concentrated effort. Successful performances whether in sport, music or art appear so unfairly natural and effortless. In rifle shooting, the perfect release of the trigger is spontaneous, automatic, like ripe fruit falling from a tree. The rhythm of the successful swimmer or rower flows in harmony with the water, the fencer 'dances' in perfect harmony, leaving everyone with the breathtaking sense of an effortless beauty. Conversely, the golfer awkwardly straining to hit the ball may build up such a state of tension, that he can't hit the ball at all; the boxer floundering around aiming blows haphazardly is out of control and in a state of tense desperation.

Often athletes ask: 'How do I know when I'm really doing my very best?' I ask them when they last entered the 'zone' and so it follows they tell me when that happened and add that only in that state were they happy with their performance.

It seems that a more objective measure of whether the athlete is really fulfilling his potential in any area is by the occurrence of the 'zone'. Very often people who ask that question have never, in fact, achieved the state. Those who have, know that at that time they performed superbly and even if they did not get a medal, they consider that personally they won. Athletes remark that they do not experience that perfect feeling too often – Olympic medallist John Treacy, for instance, experienced the state only three or four times in his career, as have other top international medallists. They all acknowledge, however, that they can remember it so intensely: 'It was magic. It was unbelievable. I didn't hear the crowds roaring but I remember that feeling.' Maybe here we have an answer to the view that 'doing your best is too vague'.

Enjoyment

Beneath the willows, singing and laughing with my friends;
this fine spring day,
Is truly full of joy.[10]

Royokan was an acclaimed poet and calligrapher. A muchloved and respected Zen master, he lived the latter half of his life in the mountains writing poetry. His life was simple, spent begging in the nearby villages, playing with the children, meeting with their friends, a life 'truly full of joy'.

When an athlete or a writer or a teacher tells me they are not enjoying what they do any more, it follows that they are not performing to the best of their ability. Only when we are experiencing fulfilment and enjoyment in our work can we achieve peak performance. It may be that we have to change something we are doing, it may even be that we are not suited to that sport or profession. Often, however, it just involves a different way of looking at things. Perhaps we are concentrating more on the idea of future success than the present task. Sometimes we have been doing too much and just need a break in order to return to our work refreshed.

When you start to achieve your best performance you will then start to enjoy your sport, an essential ingredient in successful performance in any area. The disinterested, sullen salesman is hardly likely to persuade many individuals to buy his product, just as the grumpy physician with an unpleasant bedside manner is not an encouraging, therapeutic factor in the recovery of the patient. We are finally starting to acknowledge that good performance and enjoyment go hand in hand and that people who enjoy their work may actually be doing a superior job to those who don't. In sport, therefore, it is important to find a club where the atmosphere is co-operative and conducive to good performance, and a coach with whom a pleasant constructive relationship may be had.

Challenge

> Just put thoughts to rest and don't seek outwardly any more. When things come up, then give them your attention; just trust what is functional in you at present, and you have nothing to be concerned about.[11]

The athletes I have seen have found that the idea of regarding situations as a challenge may be especially useful when in competition or training.

Apprehension is a major factor or distraction in competitive sport. Depending on individual differences this can range from mild stress to major disrupting physiological and psychological changes. It is necessary, of course, to have an adequate arousal level in order to perform well but this state must be directed and controlled if it is to lead to peak performance.

Repetition and imitation

Crippling fear of competition or of meeting a certain competitor may become the primary concern and once again actual performance becomes of secondary importance, leading to poor results. One of the sportsmen would actually feel very sick and be unable to sleep for weeks at the thought of facing a certain opponent, psyching out at a distance. In order to keep your attention on the main task, your performance, it may be helpful to regard the event as a challenging experience – nothing has changed, the external event is just the same, but by perceiving it differently your performance may alter drastically. By approaching things this way, you are eager to participate in the competition, rather than wishing it were over. Fear also stops the individual being true to his or her self. It is important to trust oneself and not to blindly imitate others. Those who truly carry out their best work put all their heart into it, and do not use stale repetition and imitation. 'When the young rabbi succeeded his father, everyone began to tell him how completely unlike his father he was. 'On the contrary,' replied the young man, 'I'm exactly like the old man. He imitated no one, I imitate no one.'[12] Loss of motivation may also occur when an individual becomes too blasé about his performance. One of the top Irish athletes just wanted to get the race over at an important competition where he was expected to win. As the Chinese sage said, 'It is hard to live long with a great name.' The athlete found he couldn't achieve his usual speed. He had concentrated more on collecting the medal than on enjoying the race. Having lost his edge, he came third, maybe in the same way as a painter or writer may lose inspiration in the artistic area, thinking only of the result and acclaim rather than the process of art.

Living in the present

> If you embrace the present and become one with it, and merge with it, you will experience a fire, a glow, a sparkle of ecstasy throbbing in every living sentient being.[13]

In order to maintain focus on whatever we are doing, it is crucial to remain in the here and now, concentrating fully on our task at the present moment. Unfortunately this is a difficult thing to achieve. It is often much easier to daydream of past disappointments or future hopes than to concentrate on our training or game. In training or studying this just means that our work is less effective than it could be – we are wasting precious time. In competitions or exams it could mean a distraction that makes us lose the race or fail the exam. How often athletes have told me how they thought of a previous shot or hit and missed their current one. Their previous hit may have been excellent or very poor, but the result is all the same – it takes the focus off the 'now', the current hit. How many more have told me how their worry about the next game caused them to lose this one? All our energy must be channelled into our present stroke or shot. Any distracting thought drains away our energy from the task in hand. Lieh-Tzu asked how a man can carry out amazing feats and was told: 'It is by holding fast to his purest energies; it has nothing to do with skill and daring.'[14]

So too in art or music or any performance: no thought of past or future performances must be allowed to intrude or the performance will be inferior. The only thing that we can be sure of is the present moment and forgetting ourselves and our gains and successes we can lose ourselves in that moment.

> Often the moon and I sit together all night,
> And more than once I lost myself among
> wildflowers, forgetting to return home.
>
> Ryokan[15]

If our life is lived this way we can be sure of achieving fulfilment and enjoyment. Equally we can be sure of producing our best work.

So success is not something we can get immediately; that is why we have to pay attention to the previously outlined concepts. If one of these ideas is missing, the athlete or individual is not performing well. It is as if these concepts were part of a Chinese puzzle; only when all parts are functioning does the whole fit together. Quick success is often a 'flash in the pan', a one-off experience. Any success which does not have at its foundation years of studying or training is unlikely to either be worth very much or to last too long. As an ancient Chinese sage, Wuzu, suggested: 'This principle of searching observation and careful listening is not something that can be done in a day and a night. That is why some of the greatest ancient adepts went through apprenticeships lasting ten or fifteen years.'[16]

Thus taking the emphasis off success and concentrating on each day's improvement can lead to the satisfaction of achieving excellence in whatever we do. This obviously does not mean that we will all become world champions or famous musicians and artists. We shall, however, do as well as our skill and talents allow. That alone is true excellence.

It is interesting to see that Zen masters were using visualisation effectively many centuries ago in combat and martial arts, and also to heal illness. In Japanese art and music there is also the idea of blending and harmonising, of absorbing oneself in the object and becoming the bird that is being painted – an exchange of energy, a channelling of spirit. I too have found that the most effective use of visualisation is with the meditation programme. When this centre of total stillness has been tapped by meditation, then this powerful energy can be harnessed and rechannelled.

Modern sports psychology

So maybe it was the Zen masters who opened the way for modern sports psychology and modern alternative medicine. They still have much to teach us. There are many excellent books in the area of sports psychology but very few deal with the crucial issues of performance in the 'flow' state or 'zone' and the ability to enter this state at will. Two psychologists who do deal with these issues are Terry Orlick[17], who discusses the concept of Zen and the 'flow' state in sports performance, and Robert Nideffer[18], who suggests techniques to enter the 'zone'.

As the importance of these ideas is realised then more use will be made of Zen meditation. I have found the Zen approach to be the most effective and it is also one of the simplest techniques because it becomes part of the individual's life and is so portable – everyone has to breathe. All that is needed is a good pair of lungs and the discipline to maintain the practice of meditation!

The following story illustrates the powerful results which can be obtained from the combination of meditation and visualisation techniques.

In the early days of the Meiji era there lived a well-known wrestler called O-nami, Great Waves. O-nami was immensely strong and knew the art of wrestling. In his private bouts he defeated even his teacher, but in public he was so bashful that even his own pupils threw him.

O-nami felt he should go to a Zen master for help. Hakuju, a wandering teacher, was stopping in a little temple nearby, so O-nami went to see him and told him his trouble.

'Great Waves is your name,' the teacher advised, 'so stay in this temple tonight. Imagine that you are those billows. You are no longer a wrestler who is afraid. You are those huge waves sweeping everything before them, swallowing all in their path. Do this and you will be the greatest wrestler in the land.' The teacher retired. O-nami sat in meditation trying to imagine himself as waves. He thought of many different things. Then gradually he turned more and more to the feelings of the waves. As the night advanced the waves became larger and larger. They swept away the flowers in their vases. Even the Buddha in the shrine was inundated. Before dawn the temple was nothing but the ebb and flow of an immense sea.

In the morning the teacher found O-nami meditating, a faint smile on his face. He patted the wrestler's shoulder. 'Now nothing can disturb you,' he said. 'You are those waves. You will sweep everything before you.'

The same day O-nami entered the wrestling contests and won. After that, no one in Japan was able to defeat him.[19]

I have used an adapted version of this visualisation technique with a high-school wresting team in the USA who have achieved some good results. One of the students, who performed particularly well, described his reactions at one of the competitions: 'My head was watching my body do things I couldn't believe.' Many of the students began to learn to let go of their 'need to win', and by adopting a focused psychological approach they were able to let their natural talent emerge.

Chapter 9

Application of the programme and results

Here were gulls who thought as he thought. For each of them, the most important thing in living was to reach out and touch perfection in that which they most loved to do, and that was to fly.[1]

Discipline

Any techniques which may be helpful to bring about a relaxed, focused state of mind need to be practised with the same discipline as that involved in physical training. It isn't much use to 'pull out' various techniques on the day in the vague hope that they will work. Consequently, the more relaxation and meditation are practised in a daily routine, the easier it is to tune into the 'flow' state on the day of the competition.

It is always advantageous to practise anxiety-reducing techniques initially when in a relatively calm state, rather than at a time of intense anxiety or emotion. The important point is that you feel comfortable with what you are doing and adjust the techniques to your sport and lifestyle accordingly. In this chapter I give ideas and examples of how the programme has been most effectively undertaken in training and in competition. These can be used as a guide and followed in the way each athlete feels is most appropriate for his or her own sport. Most of the athletes with whom the programme was used are top Irish sportspeople, but that is of no great importance. If used properly these techniques can help competitors to show some improvement whatever their level of ability might be.

The application programme can also be followed by individuals who wish to achieve peak performance in all aspects of their lives – or who just wish to deal more successfully with the stress of daily living.

Home programme

The home programme is recommended for everyone and applies to all sports. A good time to practise the meditation is first thing in the morning for five or ten minutes before breakfast. This helps to energise you and set you on the right track for the day. It can then be practised at various times during the day for another period of five or ten minutes or for a 'short burst' of a minute or two, or even a breath or two, before making a stressful phone call or in the car at traffic lights or even when walking along the street.

Do not meditate for too long and then give up. Better to meditate for a short time but maintain consistency. Do not look for the 'perfect' place which you may never find; sitting on the edge of the bath is fine, if that is the only quiet place in the house. Let the breathing become part of your way of life.

In training

Once you leave the house, the meditation can be less than perfect and the physical position can be altered accordingly – and fitted into walking, bending, pulling on sports gear or 'gloving up' (or whatever is appropriate for the sport in question). The rhythm of the breathing can be naturally speeded up or slowed down if necessary to fit in with the rhythm of the swimming stroke or running pace or the release of the arrow or whatever.

When fitting meditation into action it may be easier to concentrate on these shortened versions for stages one and two.

In training and competition

Stage 1: count from one to two (not five), i.e. count one on the first exhalation, two on the second exhalation, one on the third exhalation ... and so on.

Stage 2: shorten 'I shall breathe in, I shall breathe out' by saying simply 'in' on inhalation and 'out' on exhalation .

In competition

The night before a competition it is always beneficial to carry out some relaxation training in order to sleep restfully. Should there be any period of wakefulness during the night or any feelings of self-doubt, the relaxation and meditation training can help banish these distractions and restore a calm state of mind.

In the morning on waking, do a few minutes of relaxation and then get up and do five or ten minutes of meditation. From then on do short bursts of meditation to help maintain calmness and focus until the competition. As the competition approaches, the 'bursts' of meditation should become more frequent. Any panic, or negative thoughts can be controlled in this way – but remember to keep your feet on the ground (metaphorically speaking). Do not get lost in clouds of mysticism or esoteric thought. This is not a 'miracle cure'; as Zen masters say, this is 'ordinary mind' – a natural way of maintaining a focused state.

WATER SPORTS

SWIMMING

The most perfect race I had ever swum, my physical and mental state were in perfect harmony.

Shaunie McGrath
[Paralympic Games, Barcelona 1992]

In training
Five minutes meditation before leaving home. Short periods or bursts of meditation fitted into the warm-up session. Bursts of meditation fitted into practising starts and harnessing all one's energy on the blocks. Bursts of meditation may be fitted in before each set in the water. If necessary, bursts of meditation fitted in with swimming strokes – to correct the rhythm of the strokes, particularly in breast stroke and the changeover of stroke in the individual medley. This will also help in maintaining concentration.

In competition
Relaxation and meditation during the night prior to the competition. In the morning, a few minutes' relaxation in bed followed by five minutes' meditation. Bursts of meditation during the day

up to the time of the race. Bursts of meditation fitted into the lining up before the start. If rhythm or concentration is lost during a race, use one breath or word (e.g. 'in, out') as a trigger in the water to re-focus.

On the directive 'take your marks': as the swimmer grips the blocks and prepares to start the race – inhale; on the 'go and entry into the water' – exhale.

Control

As always, it is important to prepare well in advance of any race, and not just to start meditating on the blocks. Michelle Smith did five or ten minutes' meditation some hours in advance of the competition and then continued by using short bursts right up to the start of the race. She found that concentrating on the rhythm (stage two) – 'I shall breathe in, I shall breathe out' – helped because she found herself able to get very quickly into the 'flow' state and 'that really helped me to control my nerves before a race'. She found that in one race she didn't even notice that a top American competitor (Trina Radka, a silver medallist in Seoul) was standing beside her. She won the race (200 metres individual medley) and knocked one second off her previous best time. Two weeks later, despite travelling back to Canada, she knocked a further two seconds off her Irish record. This confirmed her coach's feeling that she had been underperforming due to lack of concentration; she is in fact a very calm, stable person, who is not unduly affected by anxiety. By using the meditation, she started to set personal best times in training, which she admitted was very unusual in a non-competitive situation.

Timing

Michelle's timing was off during the changeover of strokes in the individual medley but by using the breathing techniques she found she was able to control this problem. Several months later, passing on to the *hara* stage (stage eight), she started to achieve the 'flow' state much more quickly and observed that she was 'concentrating only on my breathing – it felt as though I was detached from my body'.

Michelle says of the uses of the technique for the 400 metre individual medley, a long race – nearly five minutes, during which there is a distinct possibility of a concentration lapse: 'You have no time to let your focus drift; if your concentration goes during this race, it is nearly impossible to re-focus.'

Shifted focus

At the Olympics, Michelle did not perform as well as we had all hoped. She had the previous night carried the Irish flag at the opening ceremony; she had injured her back in training several months previously. These may have been important factors in her performance. Another possibility, in view of the fact that she was doing her fastest times in her warm-ups that morning and felt very tuned-in, was that as she prepared to enter the pool for the race she was instructed to 'work her backstroke'. She consequently felt that she lost her focus by straining and trying too hard on what was her best stroke. She lost the rhythm on backstroke, as subsequent splits showed, and had used up her energy and begun to tire. At these crucial times it is probably best to refrain from giving – or taking – last-minute instructions.

Letting go

A problem besetting one particular Irish international swimmer, Jason McGrath, was that he tensed up as he prepared to dive at the start of the race. He tightened up instead of letting go. By using the *hara* stage (stage eight) he found it easier to 'flow' and broke the Irish national 50 metre long course breast stroke record.

His coach, Carole Walsh, whose calm, supportive personality played a very important role in Jason's performance, observed that, prior to his mental training programme, he became extremely tense before a race – watching others and concentrating too much on other people's opinion of his performance.

During his programme, he 'developed into somebody who could talk about his performance in a positive way – he used the concepts to exclude his surroundings, the noise, other swimmers, nerves etc., focusing in on himself and his breathing and attempting to do his best'. Carole felt that previously Jason, an extremely talented young swimmer, had been very unfocused, and rather than swimming to develop his potential had been driven by all the wrong reasons.

Paralympics

In the Paralympics, Shaunie McGrath used the breathing techniques successfully to overcome pre-competition anxiety, particularly when entering the swimming stadium, which he found a difficult undertaking. He discovered that when he meditated he 'invariably became more aware of why I was feeling anxious and confronted my emotions and realised what a waste of valuable energy it was'. The 100 metre backstroke he found was 'the most perfect race he had ever had'. He had prepared for that race with various forms of mental exercise alternating with bursts of meditation.

SAILING

[When in the 'flow' state] I seem to make decisions unconsciously and they are usually right.

James O'Callaghan, Irish sailing team

In training

Bursts of meditation before leaving the house. Bursts of meditation when putting on oilskins and setting up the boat. Bursts of meditation sailing out to the start. Bursts of meditation at preparatory signal. Bursts of meditation from time to time in the boat. Bursts of meditation pre-gybe, pre-tacking, pre-mark roundings, pre-decision making and to overcome feelings of boredom or distraction (e.g. created by a nearby collision).

In competition

Relaxation and meditation during the night prior to competition – if necessary. In the morning, a few minutes' relaxation followed by five minutes of meditation. Use short bursts of meditation until the race starts, getting more frequent as the race gets closer and then as in training.

Laser sailor James O'Callaghan talked about an onshore 'flow' – 'a sense which increases my concentration level and puts me in a professional mood' – but it appears to be less intense than that which he experiences in sailing. James describes a second kind of 'flow' which he can now initiate more frequently by focusing: he uses constant bursts of meditation when sailing.

Balance

'I feel in perfect balance with the boat. It is as if the boat is one side of a set of scales and I am the other and I know intuitively when to exert more pressure to balance the situation. I seem to make decisions unconsciously and they are usually right. My eyes are focused on the bow and the bow appears to glide across the water, not hitting any waves.' Both of these 'flow' states he can now initiate by focusing.

Another sailor described how he found it easier to hoist the spinnaker after meditation.

Maintaining concentration

It is one thing to maintain concentration for a very short race, but quite another to hold it for two or three hours and over the course of seven consecutive races. During that time there can be many internal and external disruptive influences. Many sailors are distracted by the sight of the boats passing them. It is important to depersonalise the boat's occupants and use the meditation as a trigger, to focus on the sailing. Several of the sailing team used constant 'bursts' of meditation to remain focused throughout the race.

Overwhelming need to qualify

In the Europa class, Aisling Bowman found that by using the focusing technique and a Zen approach – living in the here and now – she could concentrate much better and was enjoying her training and sailing more. At one point, she found that she wasn't sailing so well because she was too eager to qualify for a forthcoming major regatta. It was necessary for her to work out and adjust her competing inner voices, to stop worrying about qualifying and to make her main priority the idea of enjoying her sailing as she had been doing previously. When she readjusted her way of thinking and again began to concentrate on the process of training and sailing rather than on the results, a few days later she qualified easily.

Water drop!

Toby Bedell also found that meditating helped him to 'avoid negative and worrying thoughts. Without these, I am operating to my full potential'. In light weather he induced the 'flow' state by breathing. In strong winds, he used focusing intermittently when he felt anxiety over a decision: 'In strong winds, the feather technique (stage four) is hard to envisage due to continual spray in the face. So the feather is replaced by an imaginary (or real) water drop that must not be blown off.'

Suiting the individual

Each individual must find the stage which suits him or her the best. Toby tried all the stages but found that he was most comfortable with the feather stage:

> After starting, once I have decided on my tack, I commence using my breathing, using the feather technique. I try to let go of all conscious decision-making and concentrate solely on the feather. My eyes rest on the waves ahead. I let the boat tell me when there is a disturbance. If a disturbance is registered, I stop the meditation, correct the disturbance and commence the meditation again.

Toby describes how, before a race: 'I use the breath counting stage (stage one) at ten minutes before the start. I use the *hara* technique (stage eight) with two minutes to go. I am then set to race.'

To prepare for his starts, James O'Callaghan always focuses just before the ten-minute gun which he finds very useful.

Missing key

Irish sailing coach, Trevor Millar, who had previously coached several world and European champions, was well aware of the psychological pressures involved in top-level sport. He was therefore one of the first coaches in Ireland to show interest in these techniques. He described how, in the past, 'I always felt that, as a coach, you could help a competitor develop only so far. I now think that the key to the missing ten per cent can be obtained by using a Zen approach'.

ROWING

In training
Five minutes' meditation before leaving house. Fit breathing into warm-up exercises on riverbank and in boat. Practise meditation before starts in water.

In competition
Relaxation and meditation during night before competition. Relaxation in the morning followed by five minutes' meditation. Bursts of meditation, becoming more frequent as race start time approaches. Meditation during warm-up. Meditation while resting on oars directly before start of race.

In 1990, Niall O'Toole became the first top Irish rower to start using the mental training programme. He had already twice won the under-23 World Championships. His personality was an ideal combination of determination, discipline and open-minded friendliness: 'I'll try anything, if it works.'

He started his mental training and then entered his first competition three weeks later. Soon his starts became the fastest in the world, something he had not previously been noted for. He went on to win the World Championship in 1991 at the very young age of twenty-one.

Tuned in
Almost immediately, Niall started switching into the 'zone'. He started doing bursts of meditation throughout the morning of a competition, which became more frequent as the race approached. This kept his mind totally focused and when 'the coach and the rest of the team were talking, I was breathing'. In fact, he was so in tune with his surroundings at a race in Amsterdam that he became aware, perhaps subconsciously, that a rival competitor had made a mistake: 'I sensed that he had missed a stroke and I took off.'

Overcoming problems
Niall was able to control his mental state even when major problems arose. On one such occasion a mechanical fault occurred with his boat, while he was warming up for the race. All

other competitors were in place on the start line and Niall, racing up having fixed his boat, managed only a second or two of preparation. Despite that, he set off and won yet another race. On another occasion, in 1991, when racing against the heavy-weights, he realised he was coming second and the thought of getting a medal, something he hadn't previously believed possible, was enough to distract him. He slowed down fractionally and two boats passed him. Just one thought can cost a medal. The fourth place was still an outstanding achievement for a lightweight sculler. In Barcelona, only the heavyweight division is recognised so Niall was never really in the running for a medal. In fact, he had contracted hepatitis after the 1991 World Championships and maybe in retrospect should have taken more rest during the year.

CANOEING

Noise, distractions don't affect me if I'm in the flow state.

Irish Olympic competitor

In training
Five minutes' meditation before leaving the house. Meditation fitted into warm-up exercises. Meditation before each start, resting on paddles/oars. Breathing fitted into stroke if there is a problem establishing and maintaining rhythm at any point or just before negotiating a gate in slalom training.

In competition
Meditation and relaxation to cope with self-doubts or lack of sleep the night before a competition. Morning of competition, relaxation for five minutes before getting up, followed by five minutes' meditation. Short bouts of meditation throughout the day, becoming more frequent as the competition approaches.

Pre-start, fit in some meditation while resting on paddles. If necessary use meditation as a trigger in the slalom. This is not easy in speed races but one effective way may be by pushing breath down into the *hara* or concentrating on the *tanden* and experiencing a feeling of power.

Most of the Olympic canoeing teams are based for training in other countries; my access to them therefore was somewhat limited but was enough to allow me to verify that the problems were, as usual, similar to those of all other sports.

Strain effort

Straining to go faster, as in other speed sports, can have the opposite effect, as one top canoeist admitted to me. This can be a particularly frustrating situation because the athlete who is putting every effort into his or her performance may become disillusioned at the lack of improvement. At times like this, several athletes have found it may be a good idea to take a short break from training and reassess their motivation. What is the reason for wishing to go faster and needing to put in so much strained effort? Once we have worked this out, we can settle down to letting go of extraneous needs or distractions and concentrate on performance.

It is necessary in such a strenuous sport as caneoing to keep the heart rate as low as possible. One canoeist found that he was able to lower his heart rate after his work-out by using Zen meditation techniques. He generally felt that the breathing was settling him down.

Visualisation

One competitor used a form of visualisation in the slalom event but often, to his dismay, found himself visualising and concentrating on his mistakes. This of course would have made those very mistakes more likely to recur. Unfortunately most people seem to find it easier to dwell on mistakes and penalties than on successes. One way of overcoming this is, straight after meditation, to practise imagining yourself canoeing in that perfect state in which you can do no wrong – the 'zone'.

Trigger word

Another competitor utilised a trigger word such as 'smooth' – which he used if he did not complete a gate too well. The breathing can be used as a trigger here – for example a word associated with the breathing or an awareness of the power in the *hara* might be particularly useful.

GENERAL SPORTS

BOXING

It's all about breathing and concentration

Michael Carruth, Olympic gold medallist

In training

Five minutes' meditation before leaving the house. Bursts of meditation during gloving-up. Meditation during warm-up sessions. Some breathing fitted into sparring practice and between sparring sessions.

In competition

Relaxation and meditation during the night prior to an important fight – if not able to sleep because of self-doubts.

Relaxation training in the morning, followed by meditation. Small bursts of breathing, getting more frequent as the competition gets nearer. Any negative thoughts dispelled by breathing: in changing rooms, gloving up, sitting in the corner between rounds; when resting between periods of more intense activity in the ring – if there is time and if necessary; during any stoppage by the referee.

Over the last couple of years I have attended the boxing training camp in Bettystown with the Irish team coaches Austin Carruth and Nicholas Hernandez Cruz. Initially, as in all sports, despite the support and enthusiasm of the coaches, these ideas were not taken seriously, but gradually there developed an awareness that there was something in this approach that was of value.

Lack of training

In July 1991, Michael Carruth fractured his femur and later his wrist and was advised to give up boxing until he had had an operation. This he couldn't do if he wished to fulfil his ambition to go to Barcelona for the Olympic Games. When I saw him again in November 1991, it was with an added urgency.

He obviously could not spar and had not weight-trained for four months; as a consequence he would in all probability be demoralised by the first fight in January, two months later. I once again discussed in detail the concept of the 'flow' state with Michael, his father and his younger brother Fergal. Michael had been using the meditation for some time but perhaps not to full effect. I explained how in the Japanese martial arts it is assumed that you are more stable when breathing out and your opponent less stable when breathing in. It is important to get this combination correct. I felt that this assumption could also apply to boxing, although obviously you cannot work this out rationally. It could only therefore be achieved when the individual is in the 'flow' state. Soon Austin, Michael's father, started translating this concept of breathing into his own boxing terms.

Michael moved on to the *hara* stage (stage eight) and immediately felt a concentrated power in his legs and found this stage helped him to become more focused. He was instructed to do his meditation and visualised himself in the 'flow' state fighting all opponents and working out possible moves. When I next saw Michael on 3 January, he was very confident and describes this in the book he and journalist Peter Byrne wrote after Barcelona[2]:

> I discovered a novel way of making up for the lack of sparring and work on the pads. I would lie on the bed, close my eyes and go through my whole routine. Mentally, I visualised all the punches I would throw in – training, ducking, weaving and generally, keeping my mind sharp. To the disbelievers, it probably sounds daft but I'm convinced that it kept my reflexes sharp and my body supple during those long, anxious weeks.

Even more importantly, Michael, who was not able to spar or weight-train, would probably have started to lose confidence and get depressed if he had not felt in control of his situation.

> And as I lay on the bed with eyes closed, I fought many good fights with Billy Walsh, throwing every punch in the book and simulating conditions to the point where I was having water splashed on me when I went back to the corner at the end of each round.

The cast was removed from his arm on 22 December; everyone who has had a cast removed knows how weak the muscles feel.

> I found the therapy of immense value. And for the sceptics, consider this. Three days before Christmas, I couldn't throw

a punch, but when I climbed out of the ring after my comeback fight on 10 January, Dad said that he had never seen me toss so much leather.

After this amazing start Michael went on to qualify for Barcelona and win the gold medal.

Barcelona

In Barcelona, I was able to check constantly that the boxers were using the techniques in their sparring practice and general training.

Stress: I met Wayne McCullough for the first time just several weeks before the Barcelona Olympics. He had returned early from a training camp in Germany where most of the boxing team had experienced some stress symptoms. The president of the OCI, Pat Hickey, had asked me to see Wayne to assess his level of stress. His coach, Harry Robinson, admitted that although Wayne had coped well psychologically over the years, a mental training approach might be useful at this point. It was only at this stage therefore that the talented Belfast boxer was able to take advantage of a formal mental training programme. He responded extremely well to my programme despite the fact that it introduced to his training a totally new and different element so close to the start of the Games. As a result, he was able almost immediately to switch at will into a relaxed and concentrated state of mind.

Dynamite: When Wayne arrived in Barcelona, he continued to practise his techniques: each morning before a fight he lay down on the bed and did his meditation and felt the power fusing in his stomach. 'I knew I was going to perform well this morning,' he usually said to me after all his fights; 'I was feeling like dynamite ready to explode; my stomach felt like a ball of fire-power; I couldn't wait to get in there.'

When I checked at which point he used the meditation he answered: 'Constantly, because it's necessary to keep that level of concentration for nine full minutes, you have to be always in control; if you lose it, it's very difficult to get it back.'

Wayne also used his meditation to overcome severe pain from injuries in several fights.

I did not talk to Wayne immediately after the Olympic final in which he was defeated. I felt initially that his level of concentration was not as intense as in all his other fights, although his third round in the final was excellent. He explained to me some time later how he had left the dressing-room too early, forgetting that there would be a medal ceremony for the previous weight. He began to feel unfocused at that stage – which suggests that he was not following through correctly on his mental programme. One explanation may be that some of his family had been flown to Barcelona after his semi-final victory and this may have proved too great a distraction at a crucial time. Wayne has now joined the ranks of professional boxers and within a very short time won the World WBC Bantam Weight (1993).

Constant practice: Paul Douglas was one of the boxers who surpassed all expectations in Barcelona. He constantly practised his meditation, sitting quietly on the bus, watching the fights, and then he sat quietly meditating in the changing rooms, keeping his focus on the match. He reported that he felt very strong for his two fights against world-rated competitors and he certainly looked totally in control, so much so that he felt that the competitors backed off in the initial seconds. In the bronze medal match a taller competitor cut Paul's eye with his head with the result that the fight had to be stopped. A sad moment for those of us who had watched him fight tough bouts over the week with such dignity and skill.

Role of psychological factors not always recognised

Paul Griffin remarked about his fight when he won his gold medal in the European Championships in Sweden in 1991: 'I knew on the morning of the fight I was going to do well and when I met the Russian I wasn't at all worried.'

Paul realised later that had he continued to use the mental training programme he might have had more success in controlling stress factors in later competitions. This lends weight to the argument that an enormous amount of gruelling physical training is undertaken by so many athletes who do not always realise

the role that relatively simple psychological techniques can play
in their overall performance.

CYCLING

I stayed calm – everything was crystal clear and under
control.

Marie Eribo, Irish National Cycling Champion

In training
Meditation five minutes before leaving the house. Bursts of
meditation before the start, resting on the handle-bars. Bursts of
meditation during cycling practice to help relieve boredom and
maintain rhythm.

In competition
Relaxation and meditation during the night prior to competition
– if necessary.

In the morning, a few minutes' relaxation followed by five
minutes of meditation. Bursts of meditation up to the start of the
race. Bursts of meditation while waiting on start line. Bursts of
meditation during the race to maintain rhythm, to overcome
tiredness or distracting thoughts.

At the beginning of the Irish national championship (Cork,
1992), Marie Eribo described how, by using the meditation
techniques, she dealt with nerves at the beginning of a race. She
felt nervous but didn't panic and used the first few laps to
familiarise herself with the course. She went on to describe a
race.

Pushing the breath down into my stomach, I could feel the
sensation in my spine and the power in the top of my legs.
It was at that moment that I knew that I would do well in
the race and it was indeed my best performance in four
years.

The course did not suit Marie's style of cycling – the finish was
long, straight, flat, perfect for a sprinter, but she had not won a
sprint in four years.

On the fourth lap, Claire attacked on a short climb out of
the turn. I had just been reeled in from a previous attempt

and was feeling the effects of my efforts. Nobody chased Claire – she was fast gaining ground and pulling away from the chasing group. I panicked a little and had to chase her down by myself. This took a huge effort and my legs were screaming with pain, my lungs wanted to come up for air, but I had to push on. I couldn't afford to let her away. I would lose the race if I did. Eventually I caught her and by this stage my ribs were aching with the pain of trying to take in as much air as possible.

At this stage Marie was not in the 'zone', she was aware of the difficulty involved and was straining, but she soon switched in.

I took a breather and the race settled down again. The final lap was here already and it looked like a bunch sprint. I stayed calm – *everything was crystal clear and under control* – I was all together and flowing. I planned my position for the sprint – the race wasn't over till I crossed the line. I had come this far and I wasn't going to give in now. I picked the best sprinter in the bunch and muscled my way onto her wheel. The line was in sight, 500 – 400 – 200 metres. My legs, then my whole body started to twitch with expectation and excitement. Hold back – hold back – ready – NOW!

I came out from behind Claire's wheel and the image of training behind Colin's car two days earlier came into my head. I didn't think of winning, nor of Claire, nor of anything but sprinting past Colin's car! I crossed the line by half a bike length – I had won the national championships in a sprint. I hadn't won in a sprint for the past four years. I was champion.

Although physically stretched to her limits, Marie remained calm. She was able to assess decisions in a collected way, cutting out all unnecessary distractions.

It's in their eyes
Coach Colin Eribo, watching the progress of his wife Marie, brought one of his most talented young cyclists, Philip Collins, to try out the mental training programme.

As a coach, I could see this special 'flow' state in a lot of international riders, both professional and amateur, it was in their eyes. When I was riding against these riders I would look into their eyes and would know this guy had something I didn't have and I was going to lose.

Before Philip was introduced to this method, I would show him videos of some of the top riders and I would just say, 'Look at those eyes, Phil. Complete concentration, no let up.' I had managed to get Phil to a stage where he could concentrate fully for an entire race and get a result, but it seemed to take a lot out of him. I knew there had to be a better way. This turned out to be Zen. He was open-minded and enthusiastic and began to show results very soon. Once he knew how to get into the 'flow' state, he was the fastest thing I saw on two wheels; he was like a machine, his rhythm, speed, power, concentration – it was all there. The best ride was the 50 mile time trial national championships. I had made split times for Phil to break the record. This is what we aimed at – not winning the medal, but breaking the record. If Phil met my splits he would break the record by 90 seconds. In the first 25 miles Phil was way ahead of all my splits. For a moment I thought he was going too hard and I thought he would blow up, but I could see this look in his eyes and knew he was 'flowing'. He never looked at me, his watch, his speedo, anything, just 100 yards up the road. After the last time check, I knew he was the winner, but also he was going to take the record. I drove to the finish and stood beside the time-keepers and said, 'The record's gone.' Then Phil came over the hill just under five minutes inside the old record. It was the best time trial I had ever seen by an amateur. All the officials were gobsmacked. At the dinner dance the president of the Cycling Federation, Jack Watson, said it was 'the ride of the year'. For someone to keep 30 miles per hour up for a few hundred yards was great, but to keep it up for 50 miles was outstanding and unforgettable.

Utilising energy

By utilising all his energy in a focused constructive way instead of dissipating energy into negative thought or other distraction, Philip was able to maintain a very high consistent speed over a long period of time. He described the 'flow' state to me in the following way:

For me, the 'flow' state is a release into a true showing of the performance which you can achieve when both your mind and body coming together to provide endless control over your performance. It has helped me to control my rhythm when I am in competition, whether under pressure of constant attacks during a road race or the effort of total commitment in a time trial. Even after races, I found myself using Zen to go back and control my thoughts, my anger or joy after each race. Although I do have a lot of self belief, I feel Zen has helped to channel a belief in my body and mind, to give me an edge over all my other competitors.

At the start line I took my last few moments of thought and concentration, what came for the next hour and forty-seven minutes was a new Irish record. Not only that, but a passage of time in which *I was in total control of my body and mind*. Zen helped me to feel my way through the next hour and forty-seven minutes, *it told me what to do, how my body would react in a change in gears*. At one stage I had a problem with my position on the bike. I broke from my rhythm then settled back into the ride of my life. At the end of the time trial I found myself totally in control of my mind and body. Sometimes I have become distracted, or often cars passing could throw my mind, but this day I was in control. So much so, that in the last five miles of the race I looked at my speedometer and, to my amazement, was doing 35 miles per hour, and that was after 45 miles of one hundred per cent commitment.

Many cyclists, both competitive and non-competitive, often find a natural way of utilising their breathing as an aid to cycling. One such cyclist, Philip Harvey, while cycling every weekend in the mountainous area south of Dublin, found that he could climb to the top of each ascent without being forced to dismount when he was breathing in a natural rhythm.

Many of the competitors and coaches who have used the Zen methods have been amazed at the results obtained and often completely astonished at the speed with which these results have been achieved. It has been described as a 'secret weapon' by many but it is nothing more than perfect *concentration* – all physical and mental energy focused on the task.

ATHLETICS

When I train and race, pace is so important. The 'flow' state is characterised by rhythmic breathing which goes on to rhythm your stride and so a steady fast pace is achieved. Ultimately, the rhythm takes you over and it controls you – you are in the 'zone' – and you don't want it to end even when you are across the finish line.

Bobby O'Leary, Irish Olympic race walker

In training
Five minutes' meditation before leaving the house. Bursts of meditation during the warm-up; breathe gently as you stretch. Bursts of meditation just before every start – use it in walking and running to maintain concentration and rhythm.

In competition
Relaxation and meditation during the night prior to a race if unable to sleep or if self-doubts occur. Relaxation training in the morning followed by five minutes meditation. Bursts of meditation during the day, getting more frequent as the time of the race approaches. Meditation on starting line. Breathing in on the 'set' position and then breathing out on the 'go' to create an explosive start. In longer races, fit breathing into stride to overcome distractions or negative feelings or to act as a trigger for 'flow' state.

Everything felt automatic
Some of the athletes described when they had experienced this 'flow' state naturally, and they suggested that this was when they had really performed superbly. Some had never achieved the state at all and they were convinced that they had not yet achieved their best performance. Others, despite intensive training, had not experienced this perfect state for some time and they felt that they had reached a plateau when they should have been improving naturally, especially in view of the amount of specialised training they were putting in.

The Irish international 400 metre sprinter, Ciaran Fitzpatrick, who had last achieved this state several years previously, started to 'flow' in training within two weeks of using the programme. 'During the warm-up I felt different, really concentrated. When the session itself came, everything was very easy, there was no tightness or strain, everything felt automatic.' His times started to improve dramatically as he began to show his true ability. His brother Niall, another sprinter, felt more confident after using the meditation, a confidence which spread into his life in general. He did not notice the other competitors so much and found his times were improving.

Training sessions

Ciaran described the changes that occurred in his training sessions after only four days of practising the breathing techniques. In the performance of his warm-up drills, he noticed many differences: 'I was able to perform the drills at a much faster speed than before and felt much looser than in previous training sessions.'

He was also able to cut out any external distractions: 'It was raining but I never noticed it, my concentration was so intense ... although usually I would be constantly looking around me.'

He described the running sessions immediately after the drills as follows:

> I exploded after the start and everything just fell into place as though I had gone to an automatic gear; I was conscious of my every move but I never felt my legs tense up during the runs as would usually happen – my times were much improved. It was a complete change from the normal training session: this time *I was in control*, rather than being controlled by external factors.

Serious injuries

Training improved enormously for many people using the mental training programme. Irish international middle distance runner, Aisling Molloy, who had performed so well over the years but still had a lot of talent in reserve, found her training sessions were going better; she was more in control, more organised, enjoying her training, and doing some very fast times. Aisling had suffered some quite serious injuries and was working with Marie-Elaine Grant, the Olympic physiotherapist; she was unable to train for several months but continued with her mental training programme – meditating and visualising her physical training routine. When she started running again, she found that her times had, to her great surprise, improved.

With regard to competition stress, one sprinter found he was upset by delays before the competition. He coped with this by listening to his Walkman. When he turned the Walkman off he found that again he was distracted in the few minutes before the race so that particular method he did not feel had any long-term value. He found that by using the meditation he not only cut out distraction but maintained a focused state of mind until the race itself.

Niall Fitzpatrick described his experience as follows:

> Before going into competition, I constantly did bursts of breathing which helped me to ignore the other competitors. I was able to focus better and when running the race I was very focused and I performed well – finishing second. Despite the fact that I didn't win, I saw this 'focusing' when used correctly as a weapon for improving my performance further.

Marathon

One of the Irish marathon runners, Patricia Griffin, used the meditation while running and found that concentrating on the counting, or on the rhythm of the breathing helped her to cope with pain and feelings of boredom. (It is important to remember, however, that pain is a warning; you should not block out any pain which you feel may be different or serious.) 'In the 3 km race, I felt cool and relaxed and more patient about taking the lead. I didn't rush into the lead after one kilometre.' Several days later, in the 10 km race, she reported getting straight into the 'zone', feeling very confident, and commented: 'I couldn't be beaten – I didn't notice anybody.'

Patricia felt that she really needed to work at the meditation and results for her did not happen overnight, but she generally felt more relaxed and energetic despite her heavy workload.

One first-time runner of the New York marathon, Pam Carey, described before the race how other competitors talked about the 'wall' as they reached Second Avenue towards the end of the race. Not only were physical obstacles then to be overcome but also the psychological barrier that at this stage the runner believed she should start to experience difficulties. She found the meditation useful in overcoming this problem.

Race walking

> The result of the race became almost unimportant; I was just doing what I do best.

Bobby O'Leary, the Olympic walker, used the techniques before his start and found that he was perfectly focused and able to pace himself correctly in his walking. It is important to make decisions on how to pace oneself, when to break from the group and when to stay with them. He very quickly became able to move into the 'flow' state at will on most occasions. During the race he also used the breathing to keep a correct rhythm going and to alleviate any negative pressures or lapses in concentration.

> I enter the 'flow' state or 'zone' when I start out on a trip to a race. I can recall pleasant afternoons on trains, rolling through the countryside. I take each field, each house or whatever it may be. I take it in and just as quickly as the train window has passed it by, it's gone out of mind and so I enter into the 'zone', each thought leaving me as quickly as it had entered. I read a newspaper article or two and, again, relax – breathe and relax and the article is gone. I enjoy travelling now – each procedure, ticket buying, queuing, etc., is a pleasure of the moment and then I just move on.

> I travelled to Holland in 1992. Just before the start of the race there I entered the 'zone' or the 'flow' state and became thoughtless. Nothing that was seen registered in my mind. In the background, music played. In and out. So much so, that the result of the race became almost unimportant. I was enjoying what I do best. This is my lifestyle and I like myself for it. Ultimately, I went on to enjoy the race. It never hurt me and yet I smashed my best time by two minutes, and in the process beat the national record for the distance and beat the Russian competitor by five minutes.

PARALYMPICS (TRACK EVENTS)

The Irish Paralympic team performed very well in Barcelona and nearly all of them achieved personal best times.

Patrice Dockery's coach found that there was a 'big improvement in her starts'. She herself described her training as 'much more enjoyable and relaxed', as did John Fulham. Faster times were achieved by Colette O'Reilly at Barcelona as she became much more confident and her overall performance was much improved. Mark Berry also achieved several personal best times in Barcelona and generally performed very well.

TENNIS

By using the meditation techniques, I was able to focus fully on my game and not be psyched out by my opponents

Orla Gallagher

In training

Bursts of meditation in pre-training. Bursts of meditation in pre-serve – waiting to serve or waiting to return a serve. Bursts of meditation in between rallies. Breathe during the serve, concentrating on the rhythm or on the counting; this might take some more practice. Practise the other points to perfection first.

If still using stage one, say 'one' gently as you inhale, and automatically hit the ball on the exhalation, while saying 'two' to yourself.

If using stage two, as you breathe in, throwing up the ball, say 'in', and as you exhale and hit the ball say to yourself 'out'.

In competition

Relaxation and meditation during the night if unable to sleep or if negative thoughts arise. Relaxation in the morning followed by five minutes' meditation. Bursts of meditation during the day, getting more frequent as the competition approaches.

While walking on the court and preparing oneself for the game, do some gentle breathing. More breathing before service or while waiting to return a serve. Fit breathing into the service procedure. At the end of each point, re-focus immediately, letting go of the previous result. Use the meditation technique any time concentration lapses. Constant meditation during the changing of ends.

Only use these techniques in a competition when you have practised them in training and they are second nature to you. One of the more difficult things to do is to meditate while you are serving. Only when you can do this perfectly in practice should you use it in competition.

Orla Gallagher, who won three Irish junior championships in 1991, found she could concentrate much better by using the meditation techniques and was less likely to be psyched out by the situation and the other competitors. She also felt less likely to be put under pressure by the need to win or to please her parents and coach, a practical problem for many junior team members. She very soon had no trouble entering the 'flow' state and was unaffected by distractions.

Irrespective of the level of play being discussed, the relaxed concentrated state of mind is of vital importance. Furthermore, one of the most important factors in tennis at every level is that of consistency. After only a short period of practice, a young student I was seeing who plays for his school team in Norfolk, Virginia, reported that by using the meditation his shots, particularly his serve, became more consistent and he was more able to cope with pressure.

Likewise Elizabeth Seigne, who plays at club level in Dublin, found that the breathing techniques make her more 'energised' and provide her with more power, especially in her serve. As she breathes in she says 'in', as she exhales she makes contact with the ball and says 'out'. She reported that 'this helps pace play and generally gets it into a better rhythm; it takes a lot of practice but produces a much more powerful shot'.

PARALYMPICS (TABLE TENNIS)

I was looking down on my body, controlling it like a puppet string – heightened senses, fantastic flow.

Siobhan Callanan

Siobhan, who, with Esther Stynes, won the ladies table tennis team event bronze medal at the Barcelona Paralympics, found that she could play more consistently if she meditated while playing, and realised that if she lost a service it was usually because she had forgotten to do some breathing while serving and before the serve.

This happens in many sports. In archery, an archer ought to practise meditation in between arrows and when shooting; as soon as he starts shooting well, however, he may forget to practise the breathing – usually with disastrous results. This also happens in golf.

When in the 'zone' state, Siobhan sometimes felt as if she was out of her body, looking down on herself. This can be quite scary when it first happens and the experience should not be deliberately sought but it can happen to some athletes, as Siobhan's words indicate:

> Flow – out-of-body experience. On table feeling comes over you, know you're going to win. Automated – everything happens that is going to happen. Looking down on body, controlling like a puppet-string. Heightened senses, fantastic flow. See no one but see everything.

Siobhan learnt to switch into the 'flow' state more easily with the use of meditation. She found:

> It helps best with serves, when properly focused on bat and ball, it comes together. Other times, forehand, side-spin, serve too, as I throw the ball in the air I breathe in, as I connect with the ball I breathe out. Focus in on that serve. Slow serve, top spin, too fast to break, breathe in before. It is important to breathe out as you hit. I'm breathing post-point, I'm doing it at all times.

Another competitor, John Roche, found that by using the meditation his training improved and he was more confident in Barcelona.

TEAM SPORTS

SOCCER

Training sessions
Pre-commencement in dressing rooms. Fit meditation into intervals in training – running and practice rests. During skill

practices – any rest periods. Also match practice, five-a-side, seven-a-side or eleven-a-side. Practise breathing at any interruption in play or non-involvement of the individuals.

Match days

During the night if sleep difficulties are experienced. Bursts of meditation on morning of competitive game before team meetings and during travel to games. Pre-match warm-up as the team goes on the pitch, during stretching and warm-up exercises under instruction from coaches.

Dressing room, just prior to departure from the room. Final minutes spent in meditation quietly as a team – the opposite to tradition.

Game

At all breaks in play, e.g. goal kicks, free kicks, throw-ins, corners and particularly injury breaks where concentration can be lost. Particular players such as the goalkeeper have an opportunity during periods of inactivity to use the method – due to their position on the field which may require higher levels of concentration.

In the dressing room at half-time, during the coach's summary and advice for the second half – important not to lose concentration on objectives of the second half while players are tiring out.

> When I did my breathing it was all so simple, I knew the ball would be there, the drifting ball comes to you.
>
> David Campbell, St Patrick's Athletic

Noel, the coach to St Patrick's Athletic, felt that the meditation was particularly useful in the period just before the game. 'I think it helped to focus the unit into a state of togetherness prior to the game. This was also so at half-time.' The team felt more united, more in harmony after the meditation.

One of the major difficulties for all concerned in team sports is that many players want to do their own thing before a game. The strength of St Pat's was that they were all prepared to work together on their meditation in the dressing room. The whole team including manager Brian Kerr, coaches and physiotherapist were involved. During the meditation Brian or Noel would quietly talk them through the various types of game they were expected to play in their positions. The coach felt that 'visualising while breathing helped to bring all the team into an understanding of each other's role in the team'.

One player who had not been in the 'zone' for several months was left back Pat Kelch (Kelchie). After practising the mental training programme for a short time he felt he could switch in to the 'zone' more readily, and began to anticipate where the ball was going.

Experienced players Johnny McDonnell and Pat Dolan were particularly enthusiastic about the techniques and gave the team great encouragement in this area. Pat Dolan was full of negative feelings prior to an important match with Shelbourne at Harold's Cross. 'I was too conscious of what defeat would mean to everyone.' In the pre-game talk and meditation session, however, he found 'that the game began to focus in my mind, my fears were put aside and I genuinely believed we could not lose – we didn't'.

Not all the players could recognise this relaxed concentrated state of mind. One of the younger players Christy McElligott, who was playing very well, explained how 'I've never had that state before naturally but now everything comes into one – I can find it much easier to read the game'.

It was important to stress that the techniques needed to be practised and the majority could see the importance and agreed with a player that 'the meditation becomes more natural as the weeks go by'. Many team members felt that they were becoming less negative. They were no longer so affected by doubts and fears and as a consequence of this Ian Hill felt that he was not making so many mistakes.

RUGBY

Training sessions

Pre-commencement in dressing-room. Fit bursts of meditation into all aspects of training – during warm-up and stretching, pre-kick-off practice, scrum practice – to build up concentrated strength. Practise breathing at any interruption in play or non-involvement of individual.

Match days

Bursts of meditation during night if sleeping is difficult, on morning of competitive game. Before team meetings and during travel to games. Fit meditation into pre-match stretching and warm-up exercises. Spend a few minutes in quiet meditation in the dressing room.

Game

Prior to scrum, all breaks in play, goal kicks, penalty kicks, injury breaks and any other form of delay. Any player should use the meditation during periods of inactivity, half-time interval.

> In the final analysis it is the mental application to the game which often provides the winning edge.
>
> Ian Snook, New Zealander, Coach Old Wesley

One of the most important concepts in any sport is that of getting the player to concentrate on playing well rather than on winning. Leinster player John Feehan saw the relevance of this point and commented: 'You can't know you're going to win, but you can know you are going to play well.' When the whole team accepts this, tensions will lessen and the players will be more in control. Only some members of the Old Wesley team, unfortunately, were prepared to accept this.

Ian Cairnduff was keen to encourage the team to look at all aspects of the game, mental and physical. New Zealand has a strong tradition in focusing on mental training and the coach, Ian Snook felt that mental skills should be practised with as much attention as physical skills. 'Only then does the player build an inner belief and ability to concentrate, to focus on the task at hand.'

This idea of mental discipline was alien to many players who feel that the more noise and physical exertion before a game the better. When, however, the coach did start to use the meditation techniques with the team in the dressing-room, they were much more focused and performed much better.

One of the players, Greg Duffy found the meditation particularly useful at points in the game when he lost his concentration. Another of the players found the breathing useful before a penalty kick – this most crucial of times when doubts begin to creep in, when every eye is on the player and the weight of responsibility is a distracting burden. By concentrating on the breathing the player can calm down and eliminate the anxiety, focusing only on his task. Some of the players found a combination of visualisation and meditation useful.

With any powerful technique care is always needed. One player during a period of inactivity in the middle of a game was losing concentration. He decided to visualise himself playing on another occasion when in the 'zone' and playing extremely well. Unfortunately, in the stress of the moment, he forgot that in the previous game he had been playing in a different position. On this occasion he was able to tune into the 'zone' but reverted to his old position and consequently made some major mistakes. It is important not to be careless with any training programmes: the more powerful the technique the more care needs to be taken.

The coach, Ian Snook, found the techniques useful in preparing himself for 'important team-meetings and pre-game talks, when I needed to be in a concentrated and confident state of mind'.

FIELD HOCKEY

Training sessions
Pre-commencement in dressing room. Fit meditation into training sessions. Stretching and warm-up. Practise breathing at any interruption in play or non-involvement of the individuals.

Match days
During night before match, if sleep difficulties experienced. Bursts of meditation on morning of competitive game before team meetings and during travel to games. Pre-match warm-up and stretching. Dressing-room just prior to game, several minutes in meditation at a time.

Game

All breaks in play and particularly injury breaks or any period of inactivity to maintain relaxed focused state of mind. Half-time interval to maintain focus and confidence.

> In the dressing-room breathing together cleared the air and created harmony.
>
> Rory O'Donoghue, Glenanne Hockey Team

I did not spend much time with the Glenanne hockey team but they all responded to the methods very quickly and very well. The coach, Eddie O'Malley, saw the importance of encouraging a quiet period in the dressing-room. Eddie felt that this could be a major factor in producing a focused team who were in control of their game. On one occasion he described how the dressing-room was very uncomfortable yet the team dealt with their distractions particularly well. After the group meditation he felt that they had been much more focused. They had played more intensely and had been much more drained of energy after the game was over. On previous occasions they had played less whole-heartedly and consequently had used less energy.

One player, Ollie Nuzem, felt he was more able to let go, he wasn't straining as he had been in the past. He also felt that the team was more unified and their play more harmonious. After a short time of mental training he found he was able to refresh himself with a few moments of meditation at points in the game where he felt drained. It was 'a different spirit than I've experienced before'.

Another player, Devon Kehoe, found that with the use of the meditation programme he could block out all unnecessary distractions. As might be expected these were the times he played well.

The goal-keeper who might have long periods of inactivity was able to maintain focus by concentrating on his breathing. By this method he could remain alert and relaxed as he kept self-doubts or irritation at bay.

Reacting to other players or to one's own mistakes is always a problem. Seamus Shaw found that by concentrating on his breathing he could overcome this problem more easily.

BASKETBALL

Training sessions
Use breathing for a few minutes every morning, to focus and before practice, to prepare mentally for the workout.

Match days
Use breathing in the morning, as in training but perhaps, for a bit longer. Use during the day, from time to time, to help concentration and focus. Pre-game, use breathing to concentrate and motivate yourself, during free time, in the locker room while changing for the game, during warm-ups, lay-up lines, shooting drills, etc.

Game
Right before tip-off. Short bursts during play stoppages. During time-outs. On the foul line – to concentrate on the foul shots. At half-time. Whenever you are substituted.

> Being a shooting guard, I find that when I get in the 'zone', almost all of my shots go in the basket. It's a fantastic feeling.
>
> Kieran Darcy, Senior, Regis High School, New York City

One high school basketball player felt that the meditation techniques helped him to clear his mind of distractions. When this happened he could then concentrate on the important points in the game. He found that he could then really focus on the action on court and his coach's instructions. When he was in a concentrated state of mind he was at his best: 'My jump-shots consistently go in, I am aware of the whole picture, I know where to pass and I really go after rebounds.' Kieran took his mental preparations as seriously as his physical skills and knew that only in the 'zone' did he realise his full potential.

Only some players of the university basketball team saw the relevance of mental training and were prepared to take a disciplined approach to this aspect of their game. Those that did found it very useful and were able to incorporate it into their study techniques and exam preparation. These players found that for the first time they were able to enter the 'zone' more frequently at will. Some players found that breathing before a foul shot improved their shooting, others found that they weren't so affected by their mistakes.

These techniques are, however, obviously more effective if they are used by the whole team rather than just a few players.

Chapter 10

Conclusions

I must only warn you of one thing. You have become a different person in the course of these years. For this is what the art of archery means: a profound and far-reaching contest of the archer with himself.[1]

This is a very personal story, my own and that of all the people with whom I worked and who shared their experiences with me. It is not a book explaining how to become an 'instant expert' on anything and everything. Like all things worthwhile, it is a challenging and at times arduous journey which requires much discipline and perseverance. It is a description of how studying some aspects of Japanese culture changed my life, as Herrigel's master warned him it would change his (above).

This change was not comfortable; it would have been much easier to revert to the old familiar safe ways – living or partly living, not saying or doing anything controversial, not getting too many successful results, fitting in. As Herrigel found, however, when you start to see things differently there is no turning back, when you start to shed a little of your image and ego and refuse to say 'the correct' things, there is no return, however painful the path forward may be. One top journalist suggested a few years ago that in order to increase the attractiveness of my concepts, I would have to make them appear more complex, to disguise them with obscure clichés. That, however, would not have been possible, for it is the very simplicity that leads to the results. Overlay the simple ideas with decorative symbolism and intellectual jargon and the effectiveness fades. The important thing, I felt, was that these ideas worked, not that they sounded palatable.

Nor am I trying to write an expert definition of Zen. In any event – as has been mentioned so often throughout this book – Zen is to be experienced, not written about. It is a book which describes how I have found the philosophy and application of Zen useful in my life and I hope that others may gain equal value from it.

Eastern thought

Those readers who are especially interested in Eastern thought, may find that this account is not sufficiently rigid or disciplined and may not capture for them the true spirit of Zen. Anyone who wishes to meditate for longer periods can do so of course as do true adepts of Zen, but these ideas are for people who might give up altogether after several days of prolonged Zen meditation, for whom five or ten minutes a day, expecially combined with short bursts from time to time during the day, may be very beneficial. Individuals with whom I have worked have found that it is really all that is needed to achieve some very impressive results, both in sporting activities and in their everyday lives.

It is also true that for those who may have more serious personal problems, too long a period of meditation may be harmful, allowing unconscious thoughts to surface, thoughts which may be too disturbing and with which they cannot deal. I would for this reason stress the need, especially in these cases, to keep the meditation very short.

Universal message

As a result of my experience with various cultures I have been inspired by many of the early teachings which transcend culture and time. Their message is universal throughout the ages.

By ridding ourselves of thoughts of gain or loss, of greed or self-interest, paradoxically we can go on to obtain more from our lives. For brief moments we can tune into the energy of the universe, unite with the infinite and soar to excellence. We have the potential to shake the world with our sporting ability or we can simply touch the lives of people we meet.

Need to be open to ideas

As with any programme, not all athletes were receptive or showed interest; as with any method, this Zen programme will not work in all circumstances with everyone. Anyone who is not open to these ideas will of course be unwilling to follow the programme correctly. You don't have to be totally committed to the principles of meditation for these methods to work but you do have to meditate properly and, for instance, not sit half-heartedly. This point may be illustrated by the story of one Zen master who was surrounded by thousands of monks but, on being asked how many disciples he had, replied that he had only four or five. Many individuals are searching but only a few are prepared to look inside themselves.

Powerful aid

Zen meditation is a powerful aid to successful living if used correctly but it is not an instant 'cure-all'. It involves a great deal of discipline – that should not, however, be too much of a problem for athletes, who spend so much of their time in physical training. This disciplined approach to the meditation programme and to life is, nevertheless, well worthwhile, as Eugen Herrigel testifies: 'Those who do not know the power of rigorous and protracted meditation cannot judge of the self-conquests it makes possible.'[2]

Eastern culture

In Western cultures the achievement of the goal, the attainment of the prize or medal is often the ultimate purpose in life. The fact that this can lead to feelings of anticlimax and emptiness is ignored. The concepts of mental discipline and self-transcendence have never held as prominent a position in the West as they have in Eastern cultures.

Many years ago the archer for whom this programme was initially devised glimpsed this concept when he talked in terms of achieving 'perfection of mind' in place of the concept of winning. He found he had begun to attach more importance to shooting perfectly than to obtaining medals. Paradoxically the less he felt compelled to beat other archers, the more success he achieved.

In control

What all the athletes who worked carefully on the Zen meditation programme found was that they were soon able to trigger a relaxed, concentrated state of mind, that 'magical' state in which they produced their best performances. Over the years I discussed this 'zone' or 'flow' state with many present and previous Olympic medalists from different countries and most admitted that they could not naturally trigger this state. They also suggested that had they been able to do so they would have achieved even more than they had. Athletes using the meditation, such as world champion rower Niall O'Toole, found that they could slip into the 'flow state' as they wished. That didn't guarantee winning as Niall, who had a period of ill health after his initial win, found out. He felt, however, that if everything else was going well he would perform to the best of his ability as his mental state would not let him down – he was in control.

An important part of improving performance in life and sport is that of quelling our noisy, argumentative minds, of letting go of our doubts and fears and allowing our creative energy to emerge.

The individual who is not swayed by pride and arrogance is calm and free, has nothing to gain and nothing to lose. Such individuals may be innovative and courageous in their methods because their creativity is not cramped by fear.

Changing perceptions

The athletes learnt to enjoy whatever they were doing. By giving up their needs and expectations and by changing their perceptions they began to find enjoyment in most situations whether boring training periods or difficult competitions. Previously many of them viewed some competitions with an excessive degrees of anxiety or complacency. They rarely realised their potential on these occasions. They began to see all situations, whether positive or negative, as challenges and occurrences from which to move on to further improvement.

For many athletes an acceptance and awareness of the importance of living in the present moment began to take precedence over the obsession with past or future. They no longer worried about the last match or the next shot but focused purely on what they were doing at that time.

The athletes tried to ensure that they were sufficiently disciplined to complete adequate physical and mental training programmes. Some individuals, in fact, suggested that one way of attaining the 'zone' naturally was by adequate preparation. Most, however, preferred to incorporate all these points and felt more in control by utilising the meditation to tune in to the 'flow' state. If any of these points was missing then they learnt to realise that success would not be complete.

Flashes of glory

It is difficult to be totally present with the beauty of a child who is demanding and complaining. It is not easy to continue with integrity and feeling when we are working on some report that never seems to end. It is almost impossible to enjoy the moment when every day for years we wake early in the morning, cold and tired, to train in the pool or on a cold field with only a distant goal for an incentive.

Yet this is what we should and can do if we wish to live our lives successfully. It is not the flashes of glory we should strive for, these are often transitory, ego inflating experiences which leave us empty and dissatisfied. Rather it is those quiet moments lost in our work or happily spent with family and friends that make us contented and fulfilled.

When we finally win a medal or produce a 'perfect' child or a work of artistic merit then we realise that the most rewarding part of the process was the journey towards the goal, not the goal itself. How many times do we regret that we did not savour more fully those moments along that road?

True joy in the ordinary

In the words of the humanistic psychologist Maslow:

> The great lesson from the true mystics, from the Zen monks, and now also from the Humanistic and Transpersonal psychologists – that the sacred is *in* the ordinary, that it is to be found in one's daily life, in one's neighbours, friends, and family, in one's back yard, and that travel may be a *flight* from confronting the sacred – this lesson can be easily lost. To be looking elsewhere for miracles is to me a sure sign of ignorance that *everything* is miraculous.[3]

We cannot enter the realm of the impossible, guarantee an Olympic medal or a Nobel prize. We can, however, as Maslow suggests, learn from the great teachings and live our everyday lives more fully, finding true joy in the ordinary, glimpses of the spiritual in the mundane. Fulfilling our potential so that we are the very best we can be. Perfection of action occurs when we live thus:

> The song feels the infinite in the air, the picture in the earth, the poem in the air and the earth; For its words have meaning that walks and music that soars.[4]

Creative being

The simplicity of early Chinese and Japanese thought is still valid in all aspects of life. Just as the ancient warriors faced their opponents in combat, so today we still confront our own inner demons which hinder our progress in life. By letting go of our fears, our resistance, our all-consuming egos, we start to take the first step to that perfection of action which can allow our creative being to blossom forth. This same profound stillness and silence, this state of pure existence may also be regarded as a state of healing. If so, then when we reach this level of relaxed awareness, we may be able to harness this healing energy in order to help prevent disorders or help to overcome illness already in progress. This power does not come from us, it emanates from some sacred source but it is our own decision how we live our lives. To make one's life more meaningful and creative, to live fully and completely, to rely on our own values and principles, not to be easily swayed and not making comparisons with others – that perhaps is the essence of the way of life and the approach to achieving sporting excellence which I have sought to describe in this book.

Chapter 11

Barcelona Olympics 1992

Every day is a good day.

Zen *Koan*

I have included a pen picture of Barcelona, as many people will never have the chance to attend an Olympic Games and might like to get a glimpse of the general atmosphere at such gatherings.

Certainly it was a privilege to go to the games and it was a very necessary stage as a culmination of all the work I had done over the previous years. It was not, however, the glamorous occasion that many people might imagine. In fact, whether athlete or official, if you are doing a good job, it is a period of hard work and great strain.

Participation rather than achieving distinction

I did reflect rather carefully, as I observed the obsessional approach of many concerned, on where the early Olympic ethic had gone. The concept of psychologically and physically healthy youths working together for the aim of fulfilling the potential of the human body and mind is sadly not as prevalent as one might wish. Rather, a self-interested, materialistic and unbalanced approach to life seemed to be a factor for some athletes and officials. Taken from the point of view that medals are the sole evidence of success, then the winners at the Olympics are few indeed and great is the devastation of the thousands who have given so much of their lives to training and to hoping for glory. An important role of a psychologist in this situation is to help the athletes come to terms with both success and failure. If the emphasis of all concerned could be switched back to fulfilling potential rather than winning, maybe a return to the ideal of old values could be established.

Pursuit of excellence

On the positive side, there was the sense of a lot of people doing an excellent job and there were breathtaking occasions when people reached their potential, whether winning a medal or not. As I walked around the village, I could see one of the world's top athletes, Linford Christie, quietly signing autographs. In the dining area, the US basketball team were easily recognisable by their height. Prince Albert of Monaco came down to the dining area, surrounded by security men and women, all painfully out of place in their formal suits amongst the athletes in tracksuits and casual clothes. Across in the harbour, Crown Prince Felipe of Spain was sailing in the races. Mostly, however, I came to recognise the world's top boxers.

Opening ceremony

It was still very hot when we boarded the bus in the early evening to take us through the streets of Barcelona to the opening ceremony held in the stadium. We entered through the back of the stadium down into an area where the teams were gathered, watching on a huge screen the pageant outside. One by one the teams filed out clutching the mandatory bottles of water. Gabon, Gambia were called, Great Britain filed up the stairs in navy and white. We stood up to go adding a mass of green and grey to the many colours, out through the tunnel, lining up on the track marks waiting to enter the stadium. A decision was made to take off our scarves and wave them and as we started moving we heard a roar from the crowds as Michelle Smith emerged from the tunnel carrying the flag. We walked around waving to the pockets of Irish supporters and then turned into the centre to join the teams and watch the others behind us.

There was a small team from Iran (all male), Mongolia, New Zealand in lovely black and white outfits, the Virgin Islands in colourful costumes and Spain, who as host country got a tremendous reception from everyone. Paul Griffin called out for a Spanish hat and was given one by a friendly Spanish athlete.

We watched on the screen as the Olympic flame was carried up the hill to the stadium and passed us by. A flaming arrow soared overhead to ignite the torch and the voices of Domingo,

Carreras and Pavarotti filled the night air as the wonderful spectacle gradually came to a close.

The spectators held blue and yellow fluorescent torches which lit up at the end of the evening in the form of the European flag. They then began to throw the torches into the centre as a good-natured 'battle' began. It was actually a little scary at times as the torches burst and stained our jackets. Wayne McCullough was hit in the eye. The disciplined entrance became a mad scramble as the huge mass of people made their way as quickly as possible out of the stadium.

Respite in the Casa Alsina, San Celoni

Two very good friends of mine, Patchi and Montsi Ochoa, Spanish diplomats based at the Spanish Embassy in Dublin, who came into the village one day, marvelled at the change in the landscape as they compared the wide streets and houses of the modern village with the strip of dock wasteland and slum houses from a few years before.

On two brief occasions in the three weeks I went to the mountains outside Barcelona, to their villa, the Casa Alsina, where my husband and two children were also staying.

I first travelled on the subway to Passeig de Gracia and then by train to the delightful town of San Celoni. The train line ran parallel to the motorway which was built along the route of the old Roman road, the Via Augusta. I enjoyed the view of the burnt brown hills and small stone villages eventually arriving at the station where Montsi collected me and drove me to the beautiful nineteenth-century villa at the edge of a forest, with its winding entrance, high wrought-iron gates and old chapel in the garden.

For an hour or so I would sit on the patio beneath the cool boughs of an old *tila* (linden) tree with Niall and Montsi and drink coffee, listening to the delighted shrieks and splashes of Clare and Andrew and the Ochoa girls swimming in the pool. Then soon it was time to return through the sleepy village to the railway station, arriving into the bustling metro station, and then once more adjusting to the claustrophobic life of the Vila Olympica.

A new trend of Irish female boxing coaches!

On one of these occasions, when buying souvenirs at the subway kiosk, I met the Algerian doctor whom I had met in the
boxing stadium. He said that people in Algeria had seen me on
television at some of the fights, sitting with the coaches, talking
to Lounes Lahiani, the Algerian National boxing coach and had
contacted the TV station wondering about my role. Maybe they
thought that there was already a trend in Europe for female
boxing coaches!

A typical day

Most mornings, after somewhat restless nights in the humid
atmosphere (the 45 degree heat was only slightly eased by the
electric fans which had been obtained for all of the Irish team
through the efforts of Peadar Casey), I went down the stairs of
the house I shared with the medical team to go over my previous
day's notes, write my team report and personal diary. After that
I set off for breakfast with Joe Doran, the well-known masseur
with the Irish rugby team who, along with press attaché Dave
Guiney, was a breath of fresh air in an artificial situation. At
breakfast we would sit down at the long refectory tables and
maybe meet up for a chat with OCI officials Dermot Sherlock,
Brendan O'Connell and Noel Keating, or some of the athletes.
Then I would cross back to check the medical office for appoint-
ments. In the first week of competition, I went down with sailing
coach Trevor Millar and team manager Mick Wallace to the
harbour, one of the most attractive parts of the village, to discuss
ideas with Marc Leveque, the French sailing psychologist, and
Giles Sabin, the coach.

  Soon the boxing competitions had started and from then on I
would be spending most of my time in the boxing stadium in
the centre of Badalona, a village near Barcelona.

Security

Security was very tight and returning to the centre of the village
everyone passed through many checks and barriers. Bags were
put through the scanners and accreditation badges worn
around our necks were checked meticulously.

Late in the afternoon, the training sessions for the boxers would start again. The disciplined figures skipping gracefully up and down on the pavement outside their house or sparring while Nicholas, Austin or Sean Horkan timed 3 minutes and 45 second periods, corresponding to the actual length of time in the ring. Sometimes I would help with the stopwatch timing. Throughout, however, I constantly marvelled at how the boxers could carry out this activity in the burning heat of the day.

Irish meeting-place

Sometimes, Michael O'Brien, the fencer, or Michelle Smith, the swimmer, might arrive for a discussion after training, all of us perhaps watching Paul Douglas sitting calmly in his cross-legged meditation position, and laughing at the witty comments of boxer Paul Buttermere, 'Butsy', whose activity would finally be quietened by exertion. As soon as the training finished the remarks and laughter would start again.. When I had finished I would go up to the medical office where the physiotherapists were working, to compare notes with Marie-Elaine Grant. Over the past two years, Marie-Elaine and I had worked closely together and had found that if I was having a 'problem' with athletes who were not adequately carrying out their concentration programme, she too had observed that these same athletes had inconsistent results when isokinetically testing their muscle strength. Fortunately, we were able to carry on these comparisons at the games.

Communal eating

The restaurant was centrally located and on entry our accreditation would once again be checked several times by cheerful young Spanish students dressed in bright yellow suits. Here, shops selling the ubiquitous Kobi souvenirs and the communication offices were on the ground floor and a winding staircase led down to the huge open-plan eating area which could seat 3,000 people at long tables, where counters displayed a wide selection of hot and cold food which hopefully would satisfy the varied palates of many different nations. Memories of my mouth on fire on trips to Korea from Japan many years previously made sure that I skipped the red-hot Kimchi, but I enjoyed trying the other dishes. Large refrigerated containers of ice-cream were placed all around the restaurant and day and night these facilities were available, supplied by the Spanish organisers.

Visiting dignitaries
Constant streams of world dignitaries passed through the village during the three weeks of the games. The Irish group included the Irish Sports minister, Liam Aylward as well as the Foreign Minister, David Andrews, and his wife whom I had met at the Department of Foreign Affairs in Dublin a few weeks previously. Now we were meeting again at a reception given by Jordi Pujol, the Governor of Barcelona, in the beautiful old Catalan palace, the Palacio de San Jaime, in a pebbled courtyard, 'El Patio de las Naranjas', so-called because of the bitter orange trees growing there. For me, however, the biggest surprise was meeting Olympic Council of Ireland Secretary Ken Ryan's wife, Margaret, for the first time and learning that she and I had attended the same convent school in England many years before.

Another surprise came one morning at breakfast when a woman asked if she could exchange one of her tee-shirts for an Irish one. She explained that her relatives came from Mayo and Tipperary. She was with the US archery team and her name was Judy Rabska. It turned out that her husband was Don Rabska, the well-known US archer, with whom I had lectured at a sports seminar in University College Dublin the year before.

The boxing stadium
Tickets were allocated for all the events but I spent most of the time in the boxing stadium as they were the team with whom I had done the most work over the years. I have many vivid memories of those days.

The bus left the Olympic village for the stadium at various times throughout the day. I usually travelled on the bus with the team, quietly gauging the mood. We stepped off the bus into the searing heat and passed through the check points, ever-vigilant to the possibility of terrorist attacks, into the refreshing cool of the boxing stadium.

I relaxed in the café knowing that most of the boxers would be preparing mentally in their dressing rooms. Over a cappuccino I discussed mental techniques with the psychologist to the Nigerian boxing team. It was interesting to hear that he used much more confrontational methods encouraging them to get their adrenaline flowing, focusing on heated thoughts rather than calm concentration.

Then I would go into the actual boxing arena and walk down to seats in the coaches section where I could get a good view of the ring. Haunting music played softly in the background and the whole place had a rather surreal air as formally dressed judges and officials walked around. Although the place was full of activity everything seemed to me to happen in slow motion, the music, the cool air, the sense of relaxation intensified the 'zone-like' state. This feeling didn't last too long when the boxing started and the screams of the crowd and the sight of bloodied faces replaced the calm.

The boxing stadium was an exciting place to be during those few days. This was especially so when the whole team was performing so well at the beginning, before the excitement of the medal fights, when suddenly the stadium became the place to be.

I remember particularly the fights of Paul Douglas who boxed superbly, beating world-ranked fighters until he received a cut in the eye at the beginning of his first medal fight. At this stage the role of psychologist was transferred from that of assisting athletes to attain their best performance to supporting the losers. The winner might need help later when the glitter of the prize had worn off and the adjustment to reality was proving difficult.

Other memories involved eagerly waiting to travel back with Wayne McCullough who was always willing to talk about his mental preparation which he took very seriously. Every morning before his successful fights he described how he did his meditation and how he knew he couldn't lose. (Remember that didn't mean he would win; it meant he would box superbly. On those occasions, however, he also won.) After one early fight when he had severely strained his biceps, he told me that the pain had been unbearable. He had continued the fight with the help of his breathing techniques and won. In the same way he

was able to made a comeback in the final round of his gold
medal fight although he had been experiencing terrible pain
from a damaged facial bone. He told me later that he had not
been in that 'invincible' state of mind in the early morning as he
had on previous fights. He had misjudged the time of the
previous medal ceremony and as a consequence had begun his
fight in an unfocused frame of mind.

Tomorrow is a day like any other

The night before Michael Carruth's gold medal final, Dave
Guiney turned to Michael's father Austin and said: 'Tomorrow
will be one of your most important days.' Austin sharply replied: 'Tomorrow is a day like any other.' This was not too
dissimilar to the old Zen *koan* 'Every day is a good day', and
certainly reflected the calm determined attitude of the Carruth
team.

The gold medal was won and it was time for our return.

The end of a chapter

On our return flight to Dublin the pilot was Captain Harry
Gallagher whom I had worked with on the sailing team. I went
up into the cockpit to talk to him, leaving behind briefly the high
spirits of the main body of the plane. It wasn't high spirits for
everyone of course; many knew that they could have performed
much better and that was what they would have to come to
terms with, not the fact that they hadn't won a medal.

Looking through the cockpit window I saw lights stretching
along the Spanish coastline and I felt strangely peaceful – I
thought back to that other important plane journey many years
before on my way to Tokyo. That chapter had finally been
completed. Soon I would be moving on to spend a few years in
New York and maybe another chapter would be unfolding.

Notes

Chapter 1 The beginning of the journey

1 *Zen in the Art of Archery*, Eugen Herrigel, Arkana (1985)

2 *A Zen Wave*, Robert Aitken, Weatherhill (1978)

3 *sensei* is the Japanese word for honoured teacher or master

4 *Japan the Beautiful and Myself*, Yasunari Kawabata, translated by E G Seidensticker, Kodansha Int'l Ltd (1974)

5 *Zen Buddhism and Psychoanalysis*, Erich Fromm, D T Suzuki and Richard De Martino, Harper Colophon (1970)

6 *Zen Meditation Therapy*, Tomio Hirai, Japan Publications Inc. (1975)

7 The concept of 'flow' has been developed by Mihaly Csikszentmihalyi – see *The Evolving Self*, Harper Collins (1993) and *Flow: The Psychology of Optimal Experience*, Harper and Row (1990)

Chapter 2 The martial arts

1 *Zen and the Ways*, Trevor Leggett, Charles E Tuttle (1987)

2 *The Zen Teaching of Bodhidharma*, translated by Red Pine, North Point Press (1989)

3 *Zen Enlightenment*, Heinrich Dumoulin, Weatherill (1979)

4 *The Wisdom of the Zen Masters*, Irmgard Schloegl, Sheldon Press (1975)

5 *Zen and the Birds of Appetite*, Thomas Merton, a New Directions Book (1968)

6 *The Cloud of Unknowing* and *The Book of Privy Counselling*, William Johnston SJ, Image Books (1973)

7 *The Wisdom of the Sufis*, Kenneth Cragg, New Directions (1976)

8 *The Conference of the Birds*, Farid ud-Din Attar, translated by CS Nott, Shambhala (1993). (Note: *si-murgh* means 'thirty birds' in direct translation from the Persian)

9 *The Zen Way to the Martial Arts*, Taisen Deshimaru, Arkana (1991)

10 *Psychology and Religion: West and East*, C G Jung, Routledge and Kegan Paul (1977)

11 Words spoken by Zen master Bukko when facing death by the sword of a Mongol soldier. From *The Warrior Koans*, Trevor Leggett, Arkana (1985)

12 *One Robe, One Bowl – The Zen Poetry of Ryokan*, translated by John Stevens, Weatherhill (1977)

13 see glossary

14 *The Book of Lieh-tzu: A Classic of Tao*, translated by A C Graham, Mandala (1991)

15 *The Warrior Koans*, Trevor Leggett, Arkana (1985)

16 *A Book of Five Rings*, Miyamoto Musashi, translated by Victor Harris, Overlook Press (1982)

17 *Ibid.*

18 *Ibid.*

19 *The Zen Way to the Martial Arts*, Taisen Deshimaru, Arkana (1991)

20 *Zen in the Art of Archery*, Eugen Herrigel, Arkana (1985)

21 *Moving Zen*, C W Nicol, Paul H Crompton Ltd (1981)

22 *Karate-Dō My Way of Life*, Gichin Funakoshi, Kodansha (1981)

23 *Moving Zen*, C W Nicol, Paul H Crompton Ltd (1981)
24 *Ibid.*
25 *The Zen Way to the Martial Arts*, Taisen Deshimaru, Arkana (1991)
26 *Moving Zen*, C W Nicol, Paul H Crompton Ltd (1981)
27 *The Book of Lieh-tzu: A Classic of Tao*, translated by A C Graham, Mandala (1990)
28 *Zen in the Martial Arts*, Joe Hyams, Bantam Books (1982)
29 *A Zen Way of Baseball*, Sadaharu Oh and David Faulkner, Times Books (1984)
30 *Zen in the Art of Archery*, Eugen Herrigel, Arkana (1985)
31 *Zen Training – Methods and Philosophy*, Katsuki Sekida, Weatherhill (1975)
32 *The Book of Lieh-tzu: A Classic of Tao*, translated by A C Graham, Mandala, (1990)
33 *Kyudo: The Art of Zen Archery*, Hans Joachim Stein, Element Books (1988)
34 *A Book of Five Rings*, Miyamoto Musashi, including 'Family Traditions in the Art of War' by Yagyu Munenori, translated by Thomas Cleary, Shambala (1993)

Chapter 3 The artistic expression of Zen

1 *One Robe, One Bowl: The Zen Poetry of Ryokan*, translated by John Stevens, Weatherhill (1977)
2 *Zen Flesh, Zen Bones*, Paul Reps, Charles E Tuttle (1975)
3 See glossary
4 *Zen and the Art of Calligraphy, The Essence of Sho*, Omori Sōgen and Terayama Katsujō, translated by John Stevens, Arkana (1990)
5 *Zen Culture*, Thomas Hoover, Vintage Books (1978)
6 Honoured master or teacher
7 *Zen Flesh, Zen Bones*, Paul Reps, Charles E Tuttle (1975)
8 *Japan the Beautiful and Myself*, Yasunari Kawabata, translated by E G Seidensticker, Kodansha Int'l Ltd (1974)
9 *Zen and the Ways*, Trevor Leggett, Charles E Tuttle (1987)
10 Unpublished term paper, Margot Bohl, Sophia University, Tokyo
11 *Sumi-e, an Introduction to Ink Painting*, Nanae Momiyama, Charles E Tuttle (1967)
12 *Zen Buddhism and Psychoanalysis*, Erich Fromm, D T Suzuki and Richard De Martino, Harper Colophon (1970)
13 *Zen in the Art of Painting*, Helmut Brinker, Arkana (1987)
14 *Zen in the Art of the Tea Ceremony*, Horst Hammitzsh, translated by Peter Lemesurier, Penguin Books (1989)
15 *Japan the Beautiful and Myself*, Yasunari Kawabata, translated by E G Seidensticker, Kodansha Int'l Ltd (1974)
16 *Zen Culture*, Thomas Hoover, Vintage Books (1978)
17 *A Zen Wave, Bashō's Haiku and Zen*, Robert Aitken (1978)
18 *Zen in the Art of Flower Arrangement*, Gustie L Herrigel, Routledge and Kegan Paul (1958)
19 *Ibid.*
20 *Ibid.*

Chapter 4 The art of perfection in daily life

1 *The Zen Way to the Martial Arts*, Taisen Deshimaru, Arkana (1991)
2 *The Way of Chuang Tzu*, Thomas Merton, New Directions (1969)
3 See glossary

4 *The Book of Tea, Kakuzo Okakura*, Kodansha International (1989)
5 *Zen in the Art of Writing*, Ray Bradbury, Bantam Books (1992)
6 *Ibid.*

Chapter 5 Zen in water sports

1 *Further Teaching of Lao-Tzu*, translated by Thomas Cleary, Shambhala (1991)
2 *The Three Pillars of Zen*, Roshi Philip Kapleau (ed.), Anchor Books, Doubleday (1989)
3 *The Tao of Politics, Lessons of the Masters of Huainan*, translated by Thomas Cleary, Shambhala (1990)
4 'Meditation', 'focusing' and 'breathing' are terms which may be used interchangeably in the following chapters.
5 *The Way of Chuang Tzu*, Thomas Merton, New Directions (1969)
6 *The Book of Lieh-Tzu: A Classic of Tao*, translated by A C Graham, Mandala Books (1991)
7 *Zen and Zen Classics* (vol. 1), R H Blyth, The Hokuseido Press (1977)
8 *Zen and the Ways*, Trevor Leggett, Charles E Tuttle (1987)
9 *The Book of Lieh-Tzu: A Classic of Tao*, translated by A C Graham, Mandala Books (1991)
10 *Further Teachings of Lao-Tzu*, translated by Thomas Cleary, Shambhala (1991)
11 *Zen and Zen Classics* (vol 1), R H Blyth, The Hokuseido Press (1977)
12 *Zen Flesh, Zen Bones*, Paul Reps, Charles E Tuttle (1975)
13 *The Wisdom of the Zen Masters*, Irmgard Schloegl, Sheldon Press (1975)
14 *The Tao of Politics*, translated by Thomas Cleary, Shambhala (1990)
15 *The Book of Lieh-Tzu: A Classic of Tao*, translated by A C Graham, Mandala Books (1991)
16 *Zen and the Ways*, Trevor Leggett, Charles E Tuttle (1987)

Chapter 6 Zen in general sports

1 *The Way of Chuang Tzu*, Thomas Merton, New Directions (1969)
2 *Zen and the Ways*, Trevor Leggett, Charles E Tuttle (1987)
3 *The Zen Way to the Martial Arts*, Taisen Deshimaru, Arkana (1991)
4 *One Robe, One Bowl: The Zen Poetry of Ryokan*, translated by John Stevens, Weatherhill (1977)
5 *The Grace of Zen*, Karlfried Durckheim and others, Search Press (1977)
6 *Mind/Body Running Program*, Mike Spino, Bantam Books (1979)
7 *The Book of Five Rings*, Miyamoto Musashi, including 'Family Tradition on The Art of War' by Yagyu Munenori, translated by Thomas Cleary, Shambhala, Dragon Editions (1993)
8 Transcript from NOVA television programme, broadcast on Channel 13 WNET, New York, 16 February 1993
9 *The Art of War*, Sun Tzu, translated by Thomas Cleary, Shambhala (1988)
10 *Zen Mind, Beginners Mind*, Shunryu Suzuki, Weatherhill (1974)
11 *Zen Essence, The Science of Freedom*, translated and edited by Thomas Cleary, Shambhala (1995)
12 *A Zen Wave, Bashō's Haiku and Zen*, Robert Aitken, Weatherhill (1985)
13 *Zen in the Art of Climbing Mountains*, Neville Shulman, Element Books (1992)
14 *Zen and the Ways*, Trevor Leggett, Charles E Tuttle (1987)

15 *Zen Master, Yuanwu, Zen Essence, The Science of Freedom*, translated and edited by Thomas Cleary, Shambhala (1995)

16 *Zen and Zen Classics*, R H Blyth, The Hukuseido Press (1977)

17 *Ibid.*

Chapter 7 Zen in team sports

1 'The Grace of Zen', *Zen Texts for Meditation* by Karlfried Dürckheim and others, Search Press, London (1977)

2 *Team Spirit*, John Syer, Simon and Schuster (1989)

3 *The Art of War*, Sun Tzu, translated by Thomas Cleary, Shambhala, Dragon Editions (1988)

4 *Out of Our Skins*, Liam Hayes, Gill and Macmillan (1992)

5 *A Zen Way to Baseball*, Sadaharu Oh and David Faulkner, Times Books (1984)

6 *Psyched to Win*, Robert M Nideffer, Leisure Press (1992)

7 *Zen Flesh, Zen Bones*, compiled by Paul Reps, Charles E Tuttle (1975)

8 *Zen Essence, The Science of Freedon*, translated and edited by Thomas Cleary, Shambala (1995)

9 *The Art of War*, Sun Tzu, translated by Thomas Cleary, Shambhala, Dragon Edition (1988)

10 *Out of Our Skins*, Liam Hayes, Gill and Macmillan (1992)

11 *Tao of Politics*, Lessons of the Masters of Huainan, translated and edited by Thomas Cleary, Shambala Publications (1990)

12 *Zen Lessons, The Art of Leadership*, translated by Thomas Cleary, Shambhala (1989)

13 *The Art of War*, Sun Tzu, translated by Thomas Cleary, Shambhala, Dragon Editions (1988)

14 *The Tao of Politics – Lessons of the Masters of Huainan*, translated and edited by Thomas Cleary, Shambhala (1990)

Chapter 8 Mental training programme

1 *You Must Relax*, Edmund Jacobson, MD, Unwin Paperbacks (1976)

2 The band of muscles separating the chest from the abdomen which contracts and relaxes rhythmically to facilitate the emptying and filling of the lungs. When breathing from the diaphragm, only your stomach should move, not your chest or shoulders. In order to breath using your diaphragm allow your stomach to go out when breathing in, when breathing out pull your stomach in.

3 I have tended to apply the same techniques to a blanket concept of distractions rather than to differentiate between them in any great detail as many sports psychologists do.

4 *Zen Flesh, Zen Bones*, compiled by Paul Reps, Charles E Tuttle (1975)

5 *Zen Master Dogen*, Yuho Yokoi, Weatherhill (1976)

6 *Zen Meditation Therapy*, Tomio Hirai, Japan Publications Inc. (1975) and *Zen Training*, Katsuki Sekida, Weatherhill (1975)

7 *The Way of Chuang Tzu*, Thomas Merton, New Directions (1969)

8 *The Nobility of Failure – Tragic Heroes in the History of Japan*, Ivan Morris, Meridian Books (1975)

9 *Man's Search for Meaning – An Introduction to Logotherapy*, Viktor E Frankl, Touchstone Edition, Simon and Schuster (1984)

10 *One Robe, One Bowl: The Zen Poetry of Ryokan*, translated by John Stevens, Weatherhill (1977)

11 *Zen Essence, The Science of Freedom,* translated and edited by Thomas Cleary, Shambhala (1995)

12 *The Heart of the Enlightened*, Anthony de Mello, SJ, Collins Fount Paperbacks (1989)

13 *The Seven Spiritual Laws of Success: A Practical Guide to the Fulfillment of Your Dreams,* Deepak Chopra, Amber-Allen, New World Library (1994)

14 *The Book of Lieh-Tzu, A Classic of Tao*, translated by A C Graham, Mandala (1991)

15 *Dewdrops on a Lotus Leaf*, Zen Poems of Ryokan, translated by John Stevens, Shambhala, Centaur Editions (1993)

16 *Zen Lessons, The Art of Leadership*, translated by Thomas Cleary, Shambhala (1989)

17 *Pursuit of Excellence*, Terry Orlick, Human Kinetics (1980)

18 *Psyched to Win*, Robert Nideffer, Leisure Press (1992)

19 *Zen Flesh, Zen Bones*, compiled by Paul Reps, Charles E Tuttle (1975)

Chapter 9 Application of the programme and results
1 *Jonathan Livingston Seagull*, Richard Bach, Avon Books (1973)

2 *Ring of Gold*, Michael Carruth with Peter Byrne, Blackwater Press (1992)

Chapter 10 Conclusions
1 *Zen in the Art of Archery*, Eugen Herrigel, Arkana (1985)

2 *Zen in the Art of Archery*, Eugen Herrigel, Arkana (1985)

3 *Religions, Values and Peak-Experiences*, Abraham H Maslow, Arkana (1994)

4 *Collected Poems and Plays of Rabindranath Tagore*, Macmillan (1977)

For permission to reproduce text we would like to acknowledge the above authors, their works and the publishers with thanks. Every effort has been made by the publishers to contact the copyright holders of the above and any omissions will be rectified at the earliest opportunity.

Glossary of Zen Terms

Budo:	The Way of the martial arts
Bushido:	The Way of the samurai or warrior
Chado:	The Way of tea
Cha-no-u:	Can be translated as Tea Ceremony
Do:	The Way or Path (Chinese – Tao). The combination of the practical and spiritual training in the martial arts and other Zen-based activities is known as the Ways, e.g. the Way of the sword (*kendo*), the Way of calligraphy (*shodo*).
Dojo:	The place of the Way – where meditation and martial arts are practised
Hara:	Centre of physical and spiritual energy in the lower abdomen; see also *tanden*
Ikebana:	Flower arrangement
Kado:	The Way of flowers
Karate-do:	The Way of karate, a weaponless form of combat
Kendo:	The Way of the sword
Ki:	Breath; vital spirit or universal energy
Kinhin:	A walk performed between periods of Zen meditation
Koan:	A riddle or paradoxical problem used by Zen masters which cannot be solved by logical thought
Kyudo:	The Way of the bow (archery)
Makiwara:	A target or post for training in the martial arts
Makyo:	Visions or feelings which can arise during Zazen
Mu:	Nothingness
Mushin:	The state of no thought or detachment of mind
Rinzai:	School of Zen introduced by Eisai which invokes the *koan* as a central element
Shin:	Heart-mind
Samadhi:	The state of total unstrained concentratration or absorption
Sensei:	Teacher or master
Shodo:	The Way of calligraphy
Soto:	The school of Zen founded by Dogen; specifically the practice of Zazen
Sumi-e:	Ink painting
Tanden:	A point just below the navel endowed with spiritual meaning and power; regarded as the centre of gravity of the body. In peak performance many athletes feel power in this area. See also *hara*
Tao:	Do (Japanese), the Way
Wasa:	Technique
Zazen:	The practice of sitting meditation
Zen:	Dhyana (Sanskrit) or Ch'an (Chinese), contemplation or meditation

FOOTBALL CAPTAINS
The All-Ireland Winners
Brian Carthy

The greatest football book you'll ever buy. A unique portrait of 50 years of Gaelic football through the eyes of the players who captained the All-Ireland winning teams. Each captain who held aloft the Sam Maguire Cup from 1940 to 1993 gives his thoughts on sport and the game, memories of the glory days, reminiscences on his greatest team-mates and opponents.

Fully illustrated in **colour and black and white**, this is a magnificent record of Irish football, with ideas on team management, tactics and motivation by men who captained the greatest teams in Ireland to success. *Football Captains* captures the atmosphere of a changing game, the views, memories, nostalgia, rivalries, fulfilment and friendships associated with Ireland's most popular sport.

Brian Carthy is a sports presenter and reporter with RTE, and has established an impressive reputation in print journalism in the fields of sport and music.

ISBN 0 86327 394 7

GIANTS OF THE ASH
Brendan Fullam

A celebration of the game of hurling and the players who made it great. Interviews, photographs, team choices, autographs and players' texts for 79 of hurling's greatest heroes.

'A great hurling book ... it has the nation's history woven into it ... conversation courses through the pages as it flows through the living body of the game.' *Irish Times*

'As you open the pages of *Giants of the Ash*, you will hear again the roar of the crowds in Croke Park, Thurles, Killarney, Cork and Kilkenny. You will hear the whirr of the flying sliotar and the unmistakable and unique sound of ash against ash: if hurling were a wine then it is stored in a vintage in this book. So open wide and drink your fill.' *The Kerryman*

ISBN 0 86327 346 7

THE YELLOW MAN
Pauline Bewick

An Everyman tale of satire, with elements reminiscent of The Little Prince. The Yellow Man explores life, nature, food, drink, colour, love, dance, music, death ... With glowing paintings set to become a major exhibition in spring 1996, the Yellow Man is a fascinating, memorable and sensual creation.

Pauline Bewick is one of Ireland's most successful artists. Her work has been exhibited in London, Paris, Brussels, Italy, Germany, Canada and the USA, as well as in Ireland.

ISBN 0 86327 448 X

CHASING GOLD
Sportswomen of Ireland
Yvonne Judge

In the last decades, Irish women have streaked ahead to achieve international repect in their various fields. This book examines the historical path towards this extraordinary success, and homes in on the individual stories of the biggest female names in Irish sport – including Sonia O'Sullivan (athletics), Rosemary Smith (rally driving), Angela Downey (camogie), Catherina McKiernan(cross country running) and Michelle Smith (swimming).

ISBN 0 86327 447 1